SACRED SEASONS

Books by Beverly Lanzetta

A Feast of Prayers:
Liturgy to Holy Mystery
ISBN 978-0-9840616-7-9

A New Silence:
Spiritual Practices and Formation for the Monk Within
ISBN 978-1-7323438-3-2

The Monk Within:
Embracing a Sacred Way of Life
ISBN 978-0-9840616-5-5

Foundations in Spiritual Direction:
Sharing the Sacred Across Traditions
ISBN 978-0-9840616-0-0

Path of the Heart:
A Spiritual Guide to Divine Union
ISBN 978-0-9840616-2-4

Nine Jewels of Night:
One Soul's Journey into God
ISBN 978-0-9840616-1-7

Emerging Heart:
Global Spirituality and the Sacred
ISBN 978-0-8006-3893-1

40 Day Journey with Joan Chittister
ISBN 978-0-8066-8031-6

Radical Wisdom:
A Feminist Mystical Theology
ISBN 0-8006-3698-8

The Other Side of Nothingness:
Toward a Theology of Radical Openness
ISBN 0-7914-4950-5

SACRED SEASONS

A Year of Meditations

Beverly Lanzetta

BLUE SAPPHIRE BOOKS

Sacred Seasons: A Year of Meditations

Blue Sapphire Books website http://bluesapphirebooks.com

Cover and interior design: Nelson Kane

PUBLISHER'S CATALOGING-IN-PUBLICATION DATA
(Prepared by The Donohue Group, Inc.)

Names: Lanzetta, Beverly, author.
Title: Sacred seasons : a year of meditations / by Beverly Lanzetta.
Description: [Phoenix, Arizona] : Blue Sapphire Books, [2021]
| Includes bibliographical references.
Identifiers: ISBN 9780984061693 (paperback)
| ISBN 9781732343801 (digital)
Subjects: LCSH: Devotional calendars. | Spiritual life. | LCGFT:
Meditations.
Classification: LCC BL624.2 .L36 2021 (print) | LCC BL624.2 (ebook)
| DDC 204/.32--dc23

Printed in the United States of America

Contents

Preface

To every thing there is a season, and a time to every purpose under the heaven.

Ecclesiastes 3:1

THERE ARE, in every culture, times set aside as special, sacred days. They arrive with the hope of bringing forth transcendent moments. These seasonal rituals are designed to focus on the spiritual, and to infuse the hours with deeper understanding, truer love, and clearer vision. We might hope that every day could be like these, but soon discover that a divine connection is difficult to maintain throughout the year without consistent practice.

In this book of *Sacred Seasons*, each meditation arrives open-hearted, welcoming us to the dawning light of spirit. As a practice of soul meditations, the daily entry is akin to the bead of a *mala* or rosary, that we touch with tenderness and thread with each breath into a prayer. In its own way, the text is in harmony with the manifold rhythms that keep the holy alive, joining in the seasons of praise or lament echoing from synagogue or church, drum circle or sitting zazen. We call to our Beloved in many ways, our souls longing to be in communion with the Great Spirit of life.

The passages chosen are offered with the wish that our hearts contemplate the blessing of being born into this earthly realm of wonder, beauty, struggle, pain, and hope. Here, words soak into the undercurrent of energies coursing through our bodies, animating our attention, and opening our minds and hearts. This is the river of wisdom that washes over us and inspires us to reach for the holy silence within. For, from silence are born letters and words and sentences. Yet these are empty without the Spirit that breathes life into them. Every true meditation connects us to our Source, not to the writer or the written word but to the dynamism of God's solitude. We do not write. It is always Spirit that writes through us.

Thus, it is not my words—or any other's words—that fill these pages, but the song of the universal call of Spirit that flows through and into each of us. In some true sense, I cannot claim to be the author of *Sacred Seasons*. I place before you the words that Spirit has caused to be released through my hands, heart to heart and soul to soul.

The 365 passages have been selected from my published books, unpublished journals, lectures, poems, and prayers, and meditations posted in online forums. As daily reminders, they can be companions on your journey, little balms of comfort or inspiration, to be savored in quiet moments, connecting you to the stillness within.

The entries are arranged by season, month, and day, beginning with Winter. I encourage you to move through the pages however best suits you: sequentially on a daily basis; spontaneously opening to a page; choosing a special day, month or season; or starting in December, as the book does. Or, perhaps, when you awaken or before sleep.

There are times in life when we feel we have been touched by something elusive and mysterious, by the hidden workings of the universe, as if Spirit were reaching out to us personally. It is my hope that the meditations in this book will be another touch from the sacred, an opening into the world on the other side of the precious veil that conceals the holy and the beautiful. May each day be one of planting seeds of love. May each day's message be a golden key to unlocking the inner heart, the heart that beats as one with the Divine.

Beverly Lanzetta
Writing in the Desert 2021

WINTER

December 1

Take Our Breath, Holy Mother

Take our breath, Holy Mother.

May each inhalation and exhalation be a tribute to your glory.
May our hearts burn with the passion of your fire and your holiness.

Take our souls and use them to assuage the wounds;
may they grow stronger to hold more of your love.

Take our bodies and make them an instrument of your peace;
may our actions be worthy of your mercy.

Take us and use us, for we long to give our false selves away.
You come upon us silently and in such deep interiority that often we do not recognize your call.

And this is no wonder, since the sound of your words is so holy and the wisdom of your words is so profound that even the purest soul struggles to hold them and bear them in memory.

In silence, all that is clamoring and jarring is stilled,
and we are led to the door of your own solitude.

Amen.

December 2

The Initiation of Everyday Life

Everyday life is an initiation. It is the crucible in which your soul is fired by the flame of the Divine. You have the freedom to make of your life a mundane affair, allowing the flame within to grow dim. Or you can sanctify your life in honor of the true gift of being and the true meaning of existence. You can barter your precious human life for trifles. Or you can honor the profundity of the life you have been given. This is the method of the heart and it is a difficult, arduous path. But so resplendent with joy, suffering is erased.

Love is so purified, so much of itself, that it is the strongest weapon and the greatest force, stronger than any physical prowess. The pure heart can never be destroyed. Resistance is not strength, but weakness. Fear, self-protection arises from inner weakness. Resistance can always be countered, because it is defined and determined. But the Holy, which is dynamic and unconditional, can never be damaged. Flexibility and love are strengths. The Holy is ever renewed and never ceases. This is a truth of ultimate reality.

December 3

Humility

Humility is one of the most personally relevant and meaningful virtues. It is an orientation of great tenderness—the gentle, kind, and quiet. It has to flower in your soul. You have to breathe in its fragrance and feel the quality of being closer to the Holy, to realize why humility is the central work of the monk. Because it is elusive. It is easily diverted by self-will, by the need to be recognized, by petty complaint and judgment, by gossip and refusal to forgive, and by worldly ambition. It gathers strength when we are vulnerable, when we admit that we need each other, when we open our hearts without shame or blame, when we speak the truth—even and often especially—when the other person refuses to receive or hear the truth.

Humility is not false modesty, self-denying, or destructively ascetic. It is, instead, the consequence of experiencing grandeur—a sunset, starry night, rose petal. We are brought to our knees, our hearts overwhelmed with love, when Holy Wisdom speaks. When we encounter the words "humble" and "humility," let us remember that they are in response to awe.

December 4

Bearing the Holiness of the World

Holy, holy, holy . . . the whole earth is full of God's glory.
(Isa. 6:3)

Mysticism, if it is anything, reveres and works to sustain the sacredness of the world. Never free from the glory of the unitive vision of reality, the mystic is defined as one who feels something of the wound God feels in our human ignorance and sin, and touches something of the love God pours upon us. On the frontiers of consciousness, she or he lives with a trouble in the soul that perhaps others do not yet feel or cannot yet see. Enraptured by a love for God and creation, it is spiritual love—a love with no self-interest—in us that celebrates the Earth's joys and beauty, and works to transform conditions that breed poverty, war, and violence.

December 5

THE POWER OF CEASELESS, LOVING PRAYER

CEASELESS PRAYER harnesses the soul to God. It is recognition that we are not alone and that the world does not function on our individual efforts. It is recognition that we are connected to something greater than ourselves. Prayer lends fragrance to everything we do. There is a quality of consciousness that is tangible when a person's life is given over to prayer. Certain sweetness emerges from action that does not seek to attain, achieve, or demand. Action that arises from love, from no other intention than to love, is divine action. This is the power of ceaseless, loving prayer. This constant loving of the divine restructures our bodies, minds, and souls. It gives us the strength to bear all things.

December 6

God Alone

THE MONASTIC HEART is the flame that ignites your love; the ember burning brightly that keeps you focused on truth; and the knowledge that all loves are in essence love of the divine. When life is assessed from the perspective of history, desire, progress, possession, achievement, great honor, and wealth, the monastic heart realizes that in all this, there is one underlying fact: God alone. Everything in life can be distilled into this single realization.

December 7

Love Had Claimed Me

GAZING ON A grove of ancient redwoods, the trees whispered: *Love is the force that rules the world. See how trees offer a glimpse of love's grandeur, mountains of its endurance, seas of its expanse, rivers of its flow, birds of its freedom, birth of its awe, and death of its mystery. All creation is permeated with Love's perfume, coursing through the heart of the world, inhaled with every breath.*

How often in life do we hide that we love God; that we are devoted; that we want to be a monk. Like peace, spiritual love is a threat to common sensibilities, which in large measure depends on the failure of love to disturb convention. For isn't Love the greatest threat? Infinite Love that is made manifest in our finitude; Infinite Love that has given us everything there is to give and to whom we offer so little, so very little.

No longer can we deny Love has claimed us.

December 8

PERMEABLE SOUL

A PERSON WITH a contemplative temperament often has a pliable or permeable soul, naturally receptive to the Divine. Of course, every person ultimately has a mystical soul. But in a person born with an affinity toward contemplation, the veils between divinity and humanity are thinned. At times, such a person finds it difficult—and often doesn't know how—to distinguish between worlds, or establish boundaries with others. In the Divine, however, boundaries are not necessary. Nothing is rejected; communion between spirit and the soul is a natural flow, like a river moving without obstructions. There is no need for boundaries because nothing is false, nothing is harmful, nothing is unloving. You can be fully yourself.

December 9

The Wilderness of Your Being

In all manner of life, the contemplative person seeks truth—inexorably, even against the lower will. You can flow with or resist the movement of wisdom, but once you step on the path, you will be relentlessly drawn to authenticity. The sooner a person accepts this, the easier life becomes, because you then embrace the hidden parts of your nature, honoring your quest for meaning, and relinquishing self-harm. If you are willing to enter the wilderness of your being, the miracle of transformative grace may be yours. In this blessed state, wounds are healed, and hearts and behaviors are changed. If you have tired of your willfulness, ask in prayer or silence: "Please help me to have the strength to be truthful. Please change my willfulness to willingness." This will be more powerful and more useful than anything else you do.

December 10

Letting Go To Heal

While dying, particularly in Western cultures, can be difficult to grasp as a mystical form of healing, spiritually dying refers to our capacity for transformation and realization of our divinity. If we did not have the capacity to die, if we did not have the capacity to let go, we would never be able to understand what it means to "float in the vast ocean of being." We would never understand what it means to have a moment free from the egocentric notion of reality. It is our willingness to spiritually die that signals our ability to love, to seek truth, and to yearn for the Divine.

And because this is so, offering of the self is always involved in healing (in one form or another). Whether we sacrifice our view of reality or the way we approach disease and illness, healing requires a letting go of the attachments of the mind, and of the mental impressions the mind causes. More than deconstructive, healing evokes an offering of our hearts to be more loving, forgiving, and peaceful.

December 11

A Divine Mission

Most of us want to be recognized and accorded the appropriate status and reward for our contributions. We desire to fulfill our human potential, and there is nothing wrong with that. But the devotee has a different motivation. He or she pursues a divine mission, the *spiritual* potential that comes about with the total giving of oneself. This is a radically different orientation by which to live. It is a call to a deeper type of surrender, to recognizing the intense, personal action that the Divine exerts on our souls. It is awareness that a path of mystical solidarity with all of creation is imprinted in our beings and is working itself out through each person.

December 12

Love Creates Us

Love of Truth is at the center of spiritual life. Love seeks truth and adores the unnameable. The illuminated heart loves passionately in this way, not because we know what we are going to find or have proof of God, but because love creates us. Love sustains us. Love is the beginning. We do not love God because we want something. We love God because love is the first prayer, the first passion; love poetry gave birth to us.

When we love purely, without motive, with our whole being, and without desire for love in return, we co-create and participate in the flowing out of love. We don't ask for a demonstration, we don't demand to be healed of errors or wounds. We can make a commitment now, we can vow to love and learn to love the way Divine Mystery loves us.

December 13

Expanded Heart Consciousness

A NEW FOUNDATION for spirituality is available today. It is a mothering and feminine spirituality that is not tied to historical sins or religious punishments. It is the emergence of an expanded heart consciousness that is sensitizing us to the tragedy of our separateness, greed, violence, and pain. It is heart consciousness that rejoices in the mystical unity of life and suffers over the violation of the gentle, tender, and merciful. It is a contemplative seeing of the One in everything; an awareness of life that allows us to perceive directly into the interdependence of all realities. It is through the heart that the mystic in us comes into contact with a new life interpretation based on the unity of all creation. Even the word "unity" does not convey the vision that the heart sees, feels, and knows. It is too bland a word to evoke the wonder of belonging to all creation, from the invisible subatomic levels to the immeasurable expanse of space.

December 14

A Contemplative Ethic

THE AUTHORITY OF a contemplative ethic arises out of a mystical connection to the whole family of creation. This means that the depth of our being is in solidarity with the depth of all beings. The divine spark in the center of our soul is sustained by and has a stake in the flourishing of all other souls and life forms. It also recognizes that our spiritual life is profoundly affected by and dependent upon the spiritual integrity of every other life. We are never free from the suffering and the happiness of the world. The understanding prevalent in many religious traditions, that there is truly no individual enlightenment without the enlightenment of all beings, is mystically true.

December 15

The Silent Intonation of the All

The notion of a distant, unfeeling divinity is an antiquated metaphor. We groan with the world; we share in each other's joys and triumphs; and we suffer in each other's, and our own, suffering. The interdependence of the world is shattering to the individualistic self. We are called again and again to being-in-the-world in innermost, unconditional, love. The very nature of our bodies, of birth and death, of family and relationship, of marriage and sexuality, of prayer and devotion are highly personal, relational endeavors. Biologically the air we breathe, and the ecological homeostasis that sustains our planet reflect metabolic, physiological intimacies. Stones and rocks and water, trees and air and wind, deer and eagle and coyote, sun and moon and stars, silently intone the All. We are part of each other's matrix of being. We are meant to nourish each other, and to reflect the presence of wonder and joy. We are part of the reciprocal recycling of life's unbounded, unconditional, generosity.

December 16

The Innermost Divinity

CONCEALED FROM OUR deepest nature, we are united in a circle of compassion, we are held by an intensity of divine passion; we belong to each other and to the Holy. We are nothing but belonging to the innermost divinity. Our belonging can never be repealed, cancelled, or destroyed. No sin or error can revoke our origins. Everything that is, began in intimacy. We swim in the cosmic amniotic fluid; we are connected through an umbilicus to the Source, to the Nameless who is Intimacy Itself.

This vision of our founding impetus necessitates a revision of the stories of exodus rooted in human consciousness. We are not in exile, struggling to return to innocence prior to separation or sin, but are breathing in and living out our primary closeness in each moment. Intimacy means that our inner lives are bound to the inner life of Mystery, we share the same life, one and yet distinct. The hidden name of divinity is not infinite and all-powerful, but intimate and all-benevolent. It is not final and only, exclusive or demanding, but the relationship of longing, the love that binds us together as one, making of each moment a prayer.

December 17

Loving the Holy

Loving the Holy in all things is the beginning, middle, and end of devotion. The capacity to love without condition puts our hearts in touch with the original spark that animates creation. The miracle of love is that even if we have never received unconditional love from another person, we have the capacity to be the home of love. We have within ourselves the ability to be the source of love. Love can be our daily practice.

The prayer of the heart seeks to love how the Divine loves—to love without condition—in order to heal the inhibitions that prevent love from being welcomed into the world. In this way, you become a conduit for the Living Spirit. When you love without condition, it doesn't matter if love is reciprocated, because you have touched on the Source itself.

December 18

Loving Others Requires Wisdom

Loving inside the monastic cloister or in the still night when there are no disturbances is much easier than loving God and others on a daily basis. Loving others requires wisdom. We must be wise in order to recognize how those who do not yet know how to love, trample love. It requires wisdom to be mindful of the forces of ignorance that fracture and divide, while at the same time keeping love alive in the heart. True love is capable of holding in unity both our capacity of love, as well as our capacity of un-love. Wisdom does not require that we love to our detriment, love against ourselves, or sacrifice ourselves for unholy love. This is a misunderstanding of love.

How, then, does the Divine love? What is divine love?

December 19

Via Feminina is a Radical Path

Via feminina (the way of the feminine) is a radical path; a path of radical mercy and benevolence, a path of radical intimacy, a path of un-saying, a path that takes seriously embodiment and a return to the Divine Mother. The sins of the soul are not just personal, they are collective and historical. Mystical union must take into account the oppressions of our inner lives and of society. The path itself has to bear the suffering of those divisions. *Via feminina* is a mystical union that subsumes and bears the injustices of the world, and therefore transforms and unites them in one's own soul, healing the opposites, healing the suffering, divesting our souls of subtle forms of violence, exclusion, triumphalism, and superiority.

December 20

In the Face of Injustice

When great suffering and heartache occurs, as many families who have been separated are now feeling, the reverberation of that pain can pierce our hearts and hopelessness can sneak in. We may take all kinds of actions to try and right this wrong—to side with compassion over violence.

The injustices perpetuated on humanity, which rob us of dignity, become the context within which to revise our notions of divinity. A theology unable to contextualize the vulnerability violated by the brokenness of the world is a theology whose heart has become closed. *Via feminina* embraces metaphors of the Divine as mother, lover, and friend, who cares for and stands by the outcast, the oppressed, and the destitute. The Divine Feminine shares in our hardship and suffers with us, as we suffer whatever diminishes the spirit on Earth.

A theology of radical compassion reminds us that love entails suffering and human responsibility in the face of suffering. The events of the world call us to reorder our hearts in loving solidarity with all creation.

Today, let us pray for the alleviation of injustice and the openness of hearts.

December 21

Become a Friend of the Soul

THE DESIRE TO PURSUE the new face of monasticism—to be a universal monk of peace—is a response to the fragileness of the Earth and the alienation of our collective psyche. This call arises from the threat under which much of life, human and planetary, now endures and suffers. It is a call to probe more deeply and profoundly the capacity of the human heart, the efficacy of love as a force of transformation, and the significance of mystical participation in the building up of the world. It inquires: who speaks for the soul today? Is it just the material world? Is it just violence that speaks?

The commitment to be a universal monk serves as a counterbalance to the wanton desecration of the spirit in our midst. It is a promise to put our lives in service of the dignity of all beings, and become a friend of the soul.

December 22

Who We Already Are

One of the great mysteries of life is that we often do not know and cannot remember who we already are. So great a shroud has been placed over our intuitive beginnings, that we must struggle to find our way back to our Source.

One way to assist in healing the cause of our infirmity is to tell new stories of our beginnings. If anything is needed now, it is an awakening of our inner knowing, and of the inseparability of our lives from the generative womb that animates all of creation from within. Somewhere deep within us lies a distant light, a reflection as old as the universe itself, of our beginnings in the mother womb of spirit—a reality so radiant, original, and eternal that it appears to us as new.

We must know the truth of our beginnings to survive the tender kindness, and passionate benevolence that gives life. We suffer no absence of divinity or revoke of love; this force, this Mystery never withdraws. Our challenge is to acknowledge how much we feel and how much we know of suffering and love. Our only safe harbor is to admit the expanse of passion we have for life, while we cling in desperation—or is it faith?—to our raft of nothingness. If we keep steady, if we take up the courage to advance beyond historic conventions and religious names, we will glide toward the distant shore of an impossible hope.

December 23

THE CENTERED POINT OF NOWHERE

CONTEMPLATION CENTERS THE self not in one's religion, family, or nation, but in silence. From this centered point of no-where, all our actions and relations come into focus. As women free themselves from oppression they come full circle, recovering ancient sources of women's wisdom as tools for the betterment of their lives and their relationships. Yet, despite the fact that all civilizations posit the human as expressly capable of transcendence, this capacity to grow toward divinity is probably one of the most difficult of admissions today. If we believe in it in the private sphere, it is virtually absent from the dominant political and social realm. It is almost invariably true that in "polite" company we do not admit our desire to be saints. Our technological world has placed the divine at risk and all but made us ashamed of that superior commitment to personal holiness and human dignity that is the heart of every noble civilization. It is this reclamation not only of women's divinity, but also of the sacredness of the whole world that is urgently needed now.

December 24

The Ocean of Divinity

Beneath religious forms, and prior to their emergence, is silence. In contemplative silence spiritualities meet, forming the spoke around which theological openness revolves.

It is in contemplative silence that we know what compassion means. Here we live at the heart of reality, free from any specific theological belief. We are aware that we stand before God was God, we are in the uncreated purity of being. We are unborn. And being unborn we realize that all forms, even our most cherished religions, are but passing waves on the ocean of divinity. Struck by this sight of impermanence, we learn deeper compassion, we learn to liberate ourselves from the attachment to specific theological beliefs.

December 25

Living in God's Time

The deep self is meant to live in God's time. By resting in the holiness of time, we make progress through inaction. When we follow the rhythm of what is eternal and immaterial, we enter an enchanted universe, a freedom of being and a sanctuary of rest.

It is most important to be aware of your deep desire, of what compels you to live each day, and what draws you to the contemplative vocation. You might tell yourself, or maybe you already feel, *I want to be pure of heart. I want to be a mystic. I must know truth. I cannot abide without experiencing the Divine Presence!* Then it is worthwhile to reflect on your particular justification for or resistance to not fully giving yourself to the quest. Have you ever completely offered your life to someone or something? To the Holy One? It is also good to examine what impedes cognitive awareness of—and bringing into reality—the preciousness of life and the gifts of traveling a spiritual path. How would you go about healing?

December 26

The Monk Within

The new monastic may not be identified with a specific religion or belong to a community. Rather, such a person is staking his or her life on *yes*: the affirmation of love and nonviolence. Being a monk is not attachment to an identity—even to being a monk—but following the call within to honor the sanctity of creation and the miracle of spirit, holding the divine presence in one's heart. It is a commitment to be for the other and not for the self, which yearns to give away all that is petty, constricted, or selfish in one's heart. It is the soul's witness to the tragedies that wound our world, which offers a home for the homeless, a balm of forgiveness for human cruelty and pain.

There is no new monasticism without the aspiration of the person who yearns to be free and—in a gesture of faith—surrenders to Mystery.

December 27

THERE IS NO RULE OF LOVE

DIVINE LOVE IS non-violent, non-dogmatic, and non-absolute, because love is uniquely expressed in each situation. There is no rule of love. Love has no demand. When someone says, "You must be this way!" then that is not love. The reason the soul's journey can be difficult is because we cannot conceive of a universal force that loves us in freedom—that wants the best for us. When there is true love, when someone loves you as the Divine loves, then he or she wants the best for you.

Love heals all things. It mends wounds and soothes the broken-hearted. Love also is wise; it simultaneously recognizes both the mystery of altruistic love and the limits of conditional love. Just as God doesn't pour the fullness of divine love into the soul all at once (because we wouldn't be able to hold it), so do the wise measure love according to the person's need. Wisdom may say, "I am not able to give now." The body may say, "I cannot do more now." The wise know that certain limitations of love are gifts of compassion.

December 28

Seeds of Love

THE BELIEF THAT we do not deserve love injures our hearts; these pains perpetuate self-rejection and shame. Divine love is never absent, even when we fear its withdrawal.

In darkness, dryness, and turmoil, even when prayer is not possible, seeds of love are planted in the soul, waiting to be watered by the power of love within you.

December 29

Plea For Creativity (1)

We pass through a dark night of our collective humanity as we search for the foundation of our divinity. We are purging ancient sins or other kinds of failings, seeking within ourselves a greater truth. We know something else exists, some exuberant life which explodes within our beings. As a human community we are grappling with what it is and how to get there. In life we have glimpses of a wholeness which defies categorization and we call for it, even though it seems to have no name. Nuclear disarmament, self-help movements, war protesters, women's rights, human rights, environmental concerns, and other issues of our time cry out for recognition and for consideration of our destiny as one whole and inseparable body.

December 30

Plea For Creativity (2)

May we, as holy beings, be called to embrace wisdom—
Holy Wisdom—and to celebrate the sanctity of all creation.
Amen.

THIS COLLECTIVE INTONATION cannot be other than the plea for creativity, for belonging, for ecstasy, and for our place in the divine scheme. It is our souls that speak in darkness, crying out for recognition. It is the voice of our union with life, where we are intimately connected to all creation, which cannot withstand the separation of our collective selves. It is this silent voice which pushes aside considerations, rules, religious separatism, nationalism, karma, sin, and other human sufferings, and sacrifices itself for the redemption of us all.

December 31

The Totality of Love

MANY BEFORE US also have felt the inextricable bond of spirit-matter, and yearned for a spirituality of the whole cosmos, a global spirituality. Something—a vantage point, a knowing—was sought; a mystical awareness that all matter, all living forms, and the entire orb of existence are connected by energetic bonds of affinity. The Spirit imbues *all* life and until we come to an all-life, all-body understanding of Spirit, we will not know our true selves or our place in the universe. Spirituality is not tribal or selective, not confined to members of a privileged group, but the discovery of a reality, a principle, that governs the whole of life, like the action of atoms and molecules, or the equation of water. It is global because it is intrinsic to everything; it is not partial, selective, or fragmentary but a vision of creation as an organic whole.

Only when we experience and understand how *total* love is, will we walk the path of the mothering spirit of life.

January 1

LONGING

WITHIN ALL HUMAN situations, this flame of passion exists. It must exist, for without its burning Light, there is no creation. Therefore, as one breathes and moves, so does God within. To find Truth, to gaze upon the infinite realms of mystery, and to know the sacred, one must throw the self upon the rich meadows of Infinity's longing for Itself. Only in this way does one develop true strength.

Longing is the heart's embrace, calling forth that of which there is no other. Longing is creative freedom, the willingness to relinquish all self-definitions for one's Love. This essential call, this necessary beckoning, is both instilled from God and nourished by human intent. One must actively seek longing's melody as one would seek and master music, but simultaneously surrender the self to the movement of longing's ways.

January 2

The Three Gifts of the Spirit

TO BE AUTHENTIC is a long and lonely journey. Do not abandon the solitary path; turn inward and draw from the secret of your making, the immeasurable emptiness. Into this mix of tears and jubilation, you will pour your wishes, desires, and cares, and all that means anything to you will be given away. Do not be afraid.

Celebrate the divine words pouring forth from my life in you. Do not be distracted by the daily tumult, but stay focused on your solitary vocation. For, it is the three gifts of the spirit—humility, purity of heart, and compassion—that heal the woundedness of the world.

January 3

The Courage to Face Ourselves

It is evident that monastics—new and old—are challenged through mutual cooperation and sharing to find the means to mend the rift between rich and poor, body and spirit, and indifference and compassion. By attaining inner peace, we discover new answers to perpetual human problems—poverty, racism, ecological degradation, gender violence, war, starvation, and moral temerity. Through the witness and lives of modern saints, we can learn to direct mystical consciousness in the service of societal reform. Like women and men of faith, devotion to a contemplative ethic can be our guide to the soul's liberation from oppression. True concern for humanity and the Earth challenges us to probe our inner lives, and to uncover points of spiritual exclusion, violence, superiority, or rejection that wound our souls and diminish love. When we have the courage to face ourselves, we will realize that the true spiritual task begins in searching our own hearts for that one, holy source of unity.

January 4

The Practice of Gestation

The contemplative spirituality of *via feminina* begins with the practice of gestation. From darkness and uncertainty, it waits for the Divine to be born in its own time. The process doesn't try to contain new revelation in the dry, crusty soil of old forms, but germinates each seed in the moist openness of heart, fertile and hollow like the womb, receptive and waiting. It is the qualities of Wisdom, the Mother of all—merciful, gentle, humble, nondual, holistic, benevolent—that we tenderly bear. Verdant, womb-like theology welcomes new seeds to take root. Round and hollow in imitation of divine fecundity, gestation cannot be forced; new life cannot be prescribed. We cannot change the color of the eyes, or the shape of the nose. Similarly, we cannot fashion divine self-disclosure to our own liking. Impregnated with its seed, we simply support it, and watch it grow.

And once your pregnant soul comes to term, and the holy seeds are born, the secret door to *via feminina* will open, right inside your being. Divine Sophia has never been separate from you. She waits now. Incarnated in you—pressed into body, mind, and soul—you are an embodiment of the Divine Feminine.

January 5

THE CAVE OF THE HEART

THE FIRST AND great gift of monasticism is permission to place the eternal human longing for God at the center of one's life. It is a declaration made within one's community, but also to all the world, that we are inspired by and no longer ashamed to admit that our quest for enlightenment or divine union resides in the cave of the heart. The vows and virtues, commandments and precepts, and solitude and silence associated with monasticism are for the sake of this ideal. The whole journey is propelled by a fervent realization that in silence, samsara is nirvana, atman is Brahman, God and self are one. To be alone is to be simultaneously whole and happy, connected to the source of creation and to all of life. United in this interdependent web of relations, the monk is not for herself or himself but for the whole. In prayer, the individual sinks into that point of unity for the sake of the entire creation.

January 6

Joy

Distilled upon Eternity, Joy blesses existence, filling one's cells with the perfume of its Way. Oh Holy Sustainer, Joy nourishes the emergent souls, anointing with jubilance.

Joy's fragrance perfumes the heavens, rendering all creation delirious with Love. No words can describe this state, where one is filled with such happy, cosmic laughter, bursting from excitement and intoxicated with divine bliss.

Oh happiness, and peaceful surrender, all is well and untouched. The universe stands unharmed, ultimately fortified, as radiant and powerful Joy anchors existence to the great, melodious Heart.

Abandoned, the heart follows a Blessed Way, elevating consciousness to another plane. In Joy, all needs are forgotten and all trials dissolved, for God is at home, resplendent in the Unknown.

Joy abounds aplenty. Here upon the rainbowed heavens, there is no greater delight!

January 7

The Place of Zero

The deep self is groundless. Groundlessness is before every beginning, the place of the infinitely deep, the Deep that is also you. The true self is always before the beginning, emerging from the point of emergence. Whereas the personality or identified self is restricted by name and emotions—an entity called "self" or "myself"—the true self is limitless, formless, unfettered by images and attributes.

The true self is revealed through a continual un-formation process, or letting go of everything divisive in us. This is the universal consciousness—Great Spirit, Mystery—the place of zero. When you consent to being zero—nothing—then your whole being radiates the eternal light. Thus, a person's search for the Divine, the search for one's true self, is never a selfish, individual act. It becomes universalized in the process.

January 8

The Road to the Unknown

THERE IS A path and a journey, yet each is uniquely of one's own invention, being as varied in experience as there are those walking along its way. The similarity of paths rests not in form or in function, but in the lessons that are learned as one embarks upon the mysterious quest. Despite the many possible roads to travel, the paths all lead to the same ascent: one that will strip illusion from the mind through the releasing of doubt, judgment, cynicism, and despair. Here on the road to the Unknown the individual ego will be wrenched from the mind, replacing the small self with union in divine purpose. And here, on the lonely plains of uncertainty and the barren deserts of human conceit, will the heart be pierced with infinite mercy, compassion, and love; and the soul infused with the splendor of Divine Wisdom.

January 9

Life is Infinite Openness

THE WILLINGNESS TO confront pain is not a selfish endeavor. It is an activity of relinquishing what does not belong to God, and of being whole. One of the more profound spiritual tests is the ability to be giving, even while in pain. To know divine love, we must practice endurance, how to be in a state of abiding openness to suffering. The ability to withstand suffering is a central spiritual issue. Why is this so? Because suffering causes us to confront the distance between our conditional hearts and the divine light.

January 10

Face to Face with Mystery

Prayer is not an activity that competes with other activities; it is the basis of every activity. Work is prayer. Writing is prayer. Gardening is prayer.

Since the intention of prayer or meditation practice is to come face to face with Mystery, the unity of prayer and action is essential. Prayer purifies intentions. With prayer, no other teacher is needed. Prayer is your teacher. The inner monastery of the heart protects the silence and solitude necessary to listen for God's direct speech. This is prayer: being led into the silence where God speaks, filling you with love, unfiltered.

The monk advocates various forms of ceaseless prayer and meditation as necessary to the mystical growth of the soul. The order of the monastic day is built to harness the monk's divergent interests into an outpouring of devotion. The main purpose for living this way is to allow one's whole being to be transfigured by the Divine. Prayer can be thought of as the method the monk uses to consent to be transfigured, because prayer becomes, in essence, a vow: "I vow to be with you, always. I consent to be transfigured in you."

January 11

Inscribed By and In Mystery

MYSTICISM DOES NOT tell us when or how we will encounter the holy. This unknowing is the gripping, wrenching sorrow that marks the spiritual nights when the whole structure of the clinging self is brought down and there is no stable point of reference. The anguish of these great doubts and spiritual deaths is that there is no god ahead of the self that can dictate what and who will be known, seen, or experienced. In the moment of spiritual aridity—of a spiritual desert in which our hearts are brought against not knowing, not loving, not having—faith breaks the bonds of having to know and can just be faith, going it knows not where, being guided from an obscure luminescence, until everything just shimmers and leaves us gasping for air. In our blindness, groping in the dark, the feeling senses are heightened until one's whole being is nothing more than a mass of bliss and anguish, an ecstatic tearing and gnashing that no one else can see or hear. The dying that comes goes on "forever" until the I that ceases to die finally lets go, opens up, and is freed into the dying that is not death. After the fiery jubilation of love, we are branded by intimacy and able to withstand the intensity of being alive. There is no returning to closed doors or to close down the habit of feeling, for now one is inscribed by and inscribed in mystery.

January 12

Perfect Benevolence

In the beginning, we are swaddled in perfect benevolence. Our minds and hearts, our spirits and souls vibrate on its frequency. Every element of creation, from the smallest subatomic particle to the vast expanse of space, is infused with its radiance. Consecrated to a sacred purpose, irrevocably devoted to the Holy, the whole luminous orb of existence is attuned to the prayer of benevolence imprinted in its depth.

Perfect benevolence is the passion of divine care for creation. Creation didn't come into being in an apathetic, unfeeling way. We experience its perfection in the velvety petals of the rose, the grandeur of the elephant, or the wonder of the eye. To know our origins is to care for our selves and all creation with reverence.

January 13

The Mystical Heartbeat

IN RELIGIOUS TRADITIONS, the word "mysticism" refers to a direct experience of Divine Presence, and to the highest levels of union with Divine Mystery. It also includes the human longing for the ultimate, and the path the soul follows toward intimacy with God. It implies that the mystical quest is intrinsic to human nature—that our souls are constituted to turn toward the divine light as a plant turns toward the sun. Thus, "this condition of mysticism will never be over," because the impetus of one's entire being never rests until it rests in God. This internal movement toward divine communion—rather than our daily distraction—is the essence of spirituality. When our hearts are diverted from the quest for meaning and love, we suffer. When we experience the true longing of the soul, seeking union with the divine—we know the meaning of life itself and are illuminated by the light of peace.

January 14

Birthing the New

Birthing of the new involves spiritually dying to old habits and ways of being. Every authentic practice involves the un-formation, deconstructive process that dismantles the false self, societal distortions, and violent, authoritarian elements within human consciousness. It thus travels a unique mystical path. It includes within the purification of the soul—described variously as a "dark night," "great death," or "annihilation"—not only the release of personal illusions and errors, but also of oppressive elements within society, institutions, and religions. A seeker on this path undergoes a spiritual dismantling that exposes the hidden internal assumptions and contradictions that wound a person's cherished ideals.

January 15

The Wayless Way

THE PERSON WHO is able to enter the wilderness of the heart, who has the courage to be in the desert, waiting for the divine voice—discovers the wayless way. Here is perhaps the challenge and fear, but also the great benefit and freedom of the monastic way. The monk gives his or her life to seeking the Divine in all things; but is not tied to whether the quest has a name—Franciscan or Tibetan or Shamanic—or whether it adheres to certain agreed-upon philosophies. Rather, it is a journey—perhaps similar to the one taken by our forefathers and foremothers—to seek truth in the wild places, away from dominant cultural and religious identities.

Eckhart also describes the wayless way as "living without why," a change so complete, so elusive, so deep, that nothing in our conscious behavior can be understood at this distance outside of God. This is not merely an ideal. It is an experience. It is the experience of naughting the self, so that we become every self.

January 16

Bearing the All in All

Our journey to God is an ever-progressive penetration into greater and deeper relationships, until the self is capable of withstanding the final dissolution of identity, in which the fragments of individuality are absorbed into the interdependence of the whole. Here there is no salvation for one without salvation for us all. Our interior connections with life give rise to an existential necessity that fuels an ethics of caring, a theology of compassion, and a continual excursion into the depths of nonviolence. Intimacy defies the notion of ultimacy and absolutism. The melting away of the self, in the undoing of God and in the undoing of the world, reveals the compassion that arises from bearing All in All.

January 17

A Single-Minded Willingness

THE TRUE MONK delves deeper into divesting the self of harmful attachments and the noise of the mind. There is something deep in the human psyche that fears that if we let go of our possessions we will lack a moral compass and never repay our debt. But it is only when we find the courage to seek freedom that we understand how the root of sin or sorrow, or despair or doubt, is healed by this loving force within us. We need to confront our hidden doubt that we are not forgiven and will never be completely whole. It is compassion, not punishment or contrition that leads us to repentance and finally to love.

For not only do we want to be free from personal foibles and sufferings, we also want to be liberated from social, religious, and monastic ambition or convention. The intention one needs to follow into the heart of reality requires a single-minded willingness to penetrate what has become stagnant, staid, or unholy in one's life, to stand on one's own feet. Through a solitary acceptance of inner rightness, which is a burning ember in the hermitage of the heart, the fire of love is activated.

January 18

The Inner Stirring of Love

ONE OF THE quintessential effects of mystical experience is the overwhelming feeling of unity with and love of the Divine, people, nature, and all creation. The emotional stirring is so intense that it pierces the heart and wounds the soul. It is sensitivity toward all beings, and attunement to the unity beyond division that is felt in the person's depth. We experience that all creation is one, indivisible energy flowing into and through us. And this inner moment of the stirring of love can bring a person to tears, and usher in a totally different view of reality. The soul has been touched—wounded—in its inner nature by the energy of divine love, which manifests in physical effects.

January 19

Changing Our Perspective

We are made in love, we are made for love, we are made to be intimate with the Divine, so do not give up. Whatever we think is separating us from the Divine is not ultimate or eternal; it's only temporal, ephemeral. Every objection that we conjure is simply that: an objection from our own will. It's our rejection of love. It's a rejection of our capacity to know the transcendent through love. Thinking differently will change our perspective. It's not that we are partial and are trying to be full. We are already full and trying to rid ourselves of our partiality.

January 20

Looking at the World with Compassion

Ahimsa (Sanskrit, non-harm or non-killing), as an expression of infinite love, requires that we look at the world with compassion. If we perceive the subtle nuances that take place within relations, we will see how, on a daily basis, we create suffering. Nonviolence was Mahatma Gandhi's way of describing a life that upholds the virtues of kindness, mercy, and love. Suffering forms the basis of ahimsa, the principle behind the principle of all-encompassing humility. Because we understand suffering, we refuse to add to it.

Gandhi embraced Jesus' injunction to "turn the other cheek" to those who call themselves "enemy," because he knew in the divine there is no such thing as an enemy. The vow of ahimsa, therefore, requires practice and discipline. We know how easy it is to respond in anger or in hurt to someone who scratches the surface of our wounds. He asks us, as he asked himself, to develop the resiliency and strength that can prevent us from retaliation. Gandhi would be the first to admit his imperfection; he did not hide his foibles or fears. He shows us that no one can perform vows perfectly, but that we can continually aspire and work toward fulfilling them in our lives.

January 21

Gandhi on Prayer

Gandhi's all-consuming passion to alleviate suffering was inextricably linked to prayer—his time of communion with the God of peace. It was a daily practice that strengthened his resolve to find in nonviolence the political equivalent of the sannyasin's quest for purity of heart.

As active as his life was in service to all beings, Gandhi learned to carve out those spiritual necessities that allowed him to live in the world but not be co-opted by it. One such necessity was a weekly day of silence that he devoted to reading, writing, and prayer. As was the case for many mystics before him, for Gandhi every breath was a prayer.

From the time he was a young adult, he realized that humans are caught in a struggle between two different ways of life. One is directed toward love of the Divine. One is directed toward love of the self. While these two ways can interact—love of the Divine does not negate love of the self—there must be a priority of intention. If attention is placed on love of God alone, a person will automatically come to love one's self in the way of truth, not from egocentric desire.

January 22

Contemplation is Accessible to All

ONE OF THE seminal insights of the new monastic movement is that contemplation is accessible to all humanity. Emerging from its historical confinement to cloister, tradition, one gender, or an exclusive hierarchy, today contemplation is cultivated in daily life and decision-making. Since contemplation refers to the inner presence of divinity in one's life, it occupies a unique role in the formation of monastic consciousness. Our understanding of the intimate relationship between our emotions, brain, psyche, and spirit increasingly enriches us.

Another revision in the understanding of monasticism is its embeddedness in everyday situations. Rather than placing revelation or the advent of new spiritual paradigms outside of history in a transcendent deity, the mystical heart of new monasticism seeks to recover the sacred function of humanity through our being-in-the-world. This renewed understanding of contemplation emphasizes the participatory nature and mutuality of spirit and mind, and the integral necessity of divine-human cooperation in the building of a new Earth. It recognizes humanity's essential ontological function: we are beings who co-create the world. Our capacity to co-create may, in fact, be our fundamental anthropological imperative.

January 23

Healing Injustice

Healing the many types of injustice that exist on our planet is another essential dimension of an embodied, monastic spirituality. Of necessity, today we must integrate and understand how violations of race, gender, sexual difference, religious belief, and charity wound the soul. Further, our concern extends to the suffering of the planet, injury to life forms, and violence caused by religious superiority, national self-interest, poverty, homelessness, starvation, and war. Any authentic spirituality takes into account how the rejection of difference—as the despised "other"—has distorted the heart of the world. Today we know that the variety of life on Earth is not only evidence of the interdependence of spirit and matter, but also of the Divine Presence in creation.

Our journey of spirit honors the divine imprint in creation and the crucial contribution every living element makes toward the building of the sacred reality we call "Earth." Without rocks and trees, water and air, coyote and deer, lilies and daffodils, whales and cuttlefish, quarks and protons, our bodies and our souls would not survive.

January 24

Methodology of the Heart

THE DIVINE HEART belongs to God alone, and does not adhere to any creed, religion, or sect. It is the light that shines through life's veils, calling us to something more. We know something more is possible, and we yearn for it, for total, pure communion. As the foundation of every spiritual quest, the method of the heart is a force that gives one the strength to proceed along the arduous path that lies ahead.

The method of the heart is intrinsic to our natures. We never can be diverted from love's sacred way, which follows a pattern of spiritual growth that is more interior than emotion and deeper than the conscious mind. For the path of the heart does not follow our dictates, but only its own Way.

The Heart is quiet. It is non-aggressive, silent, and gentle. It is subtle, and its wisdom cannot be heard above the daily noise and distraction. It is so peaceful that if we really listened to the heart we would be incapable of violence and war, incapable of harm. To embark on this path you have to be a pioneer willing to ask questions and to challenge time-honored or conventional truths, because the mystical heart answers to no one but God within.

January 25

A Tapestry of Belonging

THE DIVINE SPARK in each thing is visible to the heart—the shining grandeur of Mystery here, now, shows us that all of creation is so many veils concealing God's presence. We are not abandoned or rejected. Separated by the thinnest of veils are little gossamer threads of spirit, binding us together in a tapestry of belonging everywhere present. The heart recognizes that this vision is not an approximation of what could be but the hidden unity within everything. The heart feels first and foremost the holy spark that animates everything. It cannot eliminate or suppress this sight.

January 26

To be Grateful for the Call

Drawn into another dimension of the inner life, the wayless path requires that you accept—in the depth of your being—wholly, completely, in vulnerability and surrender, the birth of the Divine and the transformation of love in your soul. To follow the call and surrender to wisdom greater than your own—abandoning intellectual pride and emotional resistance—is the path of the contemplative. To be grateful for the call, for the preciousness of this life, for traveling the path of the mystics and saints, and yearning for the Divine: This is really being at home.

When a person reaches into his or her depth, the pathless path is revealed because it is already imprinted in consciousness. Core structures and techniques of the spiritual life are present in every person's depth, even as their expression is uniquely individual. When we have the courage to enter the dark regions, a new spirituality finds its way into our hearts. At the same time, this personal revealing is connected to the mystical well of every religion and to universal spiritual values.

January 27

To Know the World as God Knows Us

MYSTICALLY WE CONTAIN the spiritual organs to directly perceive the hidden connectedness of life and to deeply *know* and empathize with the desert experience that penetrates into the religious archetypes of other traditions. This capacity to experience compassion for others and to identify with others' wounds translates into a desire to alleviate the suffering that religious divisiveness has caused in our world. To know the world as God knows us, is to risk the illusion of a separate and independent self.

January 28

Being at Home

For many mystical souls, desert spirituality represents the primordial place, the quickening moment of radical openness that initiates the upwelling of God in our depth. Here—empty of images and detached from possessions—we return to the advent of religious consciousness, the nameless source of every word and name, and the free and unencumbered darkness where Spirit gives birth in us. The person on this path is able to perceive and identify with multiple religious expressions, holding plural worlds in a unified whole. This feeling of being "at home" proceeds from the mystical genesis in our souls, into the realm of word and symbol, and is a divine-human co-gestating and co-birthing of an original and creative contemplative spirituality for our time.

January 29

IN THE FACE OF UNBRIDLED BEAUTY

WE ARE CALLED to radical openness toward all religions, out of humility for the vastness of life, and because, as the Jewish mystical text *Zohar* says, "everything is part of divinity." Radical openness is not a name for God. It is a condition of being in the world that is necessary in order to bear (in the world) the divinity of creation. As a spiritual practice it can never be absolutely achieved or made fully transparent. Rather, it is a spiritual orientation that strengthens our ability to withstand the intimacy of life, and the inevitable loss of identity that makes the self tremble and lays the heart bare.

It is far easier to have clear and concrete solutions; it is tidier to have a God that is susceptible to logic and reason; it is safer to exist within the boundaries of one's self-defined theological limits. But, radical openness makes us vulnerable; it commands an awareness that protests all polite attempts at distancing the cries of the "other."

Radical openness calls us to reverential awe in the face of the unbridled beauty and generosity of life. It is a discipline that seeks to remain literate in the things of the heart: to bear wounding and betrayal but to disallow retaliation and retribution. Radical openness beckons us to never close the door on the world, on each other, or on God.

January 30

The Monastic Impulse

THE LONGING FOR God does not require a monk's robe or ascetic practice or even community. It is imprinted in the soul as its first prayer. It is the quest for the Absolute, which burns like fire in a person's being and will not be quenched until the longing is heeded. And so, the monastic impulse is intrinsic to the human heart. It is imbedded in our spiritual DNA, forming our souls, personalities, and orientations to the world.

This development, which offers a monastic way of life for anyone, including the uncloistered and the religiously unattached, grows out of silence itself. For in meditative awareness, we discover the radical emptiness that is more primordial than religious identity—being Christian, Jewish, Buddhist, Hindu, etc. We are called to plant the seeds of a new kind of devotion, one that is open to people of religious, nonreligious, and spiritual orientations.

If the monastic orders as we know them are in danger of becoming obsolete, the archetype of the monk within us is not.

January 31

How Do We Live Each Day?

When we have a sense of the true nature of reality—whether it's in a moment of walking in the woods or in a transcendent mystical experience, or any of the other life experiences that bring us out of the ordinary frame of reference—we begin to understand that life is truly profound and sacred and that it is our duty to live life directed toward the goal of the unity of life. How do we live each day bringing unity and peace? How do we deal with relationships and social situations from a place of recognizing God's presence in everything? It is, of course, a lifelong endeavor. It's not an easy thing to do, but it puts the focus on how we as humans are asked to be co-creators with the Divine in building a new world.

February 1

Even When We Do Not Know We are Praying

All life is prayer. Plants, animals, and stars participate in a symphony of devotion, each yearning toward its Source.

Walking in the hills we watch nature praying: the falcon making circles in the air, a heron strolling through a vineyard, and the song of the Blue Oak's leaves rustling in the wind. The daily activity of butterflies and ants, sea urchins and manatees, wolves and deer are distinctive prayer forms. A family gathering for a festive meal becomes a collective prayer, celebrating the bounty of the Fall harvest.

From the moment of birth, until death stills our breath, each human heart, each soul, recites a ceaseless prayer, the very existence of our spirit in physical form is an invocation toward the Divine.

So, lie down on the Earth, feel the soil pulsing, the ants humming, the gophers digging. Are these not prayers? So, too, are the kettle on the stove, and the casserole in the oven, the dishes being washed, and the dog being fed.

Give us all your prayers, O Holy Life!! Even when we do not know we are praying, the universe is praying in us.

February 2

A Sacred Community

GLOBAL SPIRITUALITY WORKS to sustain a sacred community on Earth by bringing the voice of the spirit to matters of common economic, political, ethical, and religious affairs. As engaged practice, global spirituality is an orientation toward life that is concerned about the sacredness of, and reverence for, all human and nonhuman life; deeply committed to how social, political, religious, and economic institutions can be in service of the divinity of the world; and founded on the locus of the spirit, where there is absent a sense of "I" and "mine."

February 3

A Divine Desire

OVER THE COURSE of history, saints and prophets have spoken out against injustice and have given their lives to help sufferers. But today, a critically different and stronger emphasis on spiritual engagement with the world—termed "social mysticism" or "engaged contemplation"—has become prominent. An important and overlooked resource in most cultural indicators is that exerted by monks and the contemplative lives of religious leaders, who have been a driving force behind some of the world's most important political and social achievements.

Social mysticism applies the deep experiences of faith to the struggle for dignity and human rights. The social mystic approaches the world's injustices through the lens of the Divine. He or she is involved in a kind of messianic longing to see society transformed, whereby the personal spiritual journey is transposed into the national and international realm. His or her intention, therefore, does not refer only to action for social change, but to awareness that this action is the fulfillment of a divine desire.

February 4

THE SCANDAL OF THE MONASTIC LIFE

THE MOST ASTOUNDING thing about the interior life is accepting that you are beloved and cared for by the Divine. There is a force of consciousness working in you for the good. This is the scandal of the monastic life—not asceticism, not nonattachment—that we are the recipients of Divine Love, continually.

Because monasticism is often counter to how we live out our lives, its radically uplifting perspective can be unsettling, challenging how and why we do things. Even the degree to which we have learned to surrender and to give up our will, there is more. There is always that mysterious capacity for intimacy, which will never be exhausted.

February 5

Divine Rest

IN THE SPIRITUAL traditions we talk about active and passive contemplation. Active contemplation refers to everything we do to bring ourselves closer to God—meditative practices, study, prayer. Passive contemplation is not the absence of a positive motion. Rather, it is the action of the Divine in your being. It is God's work in you. It is here that we surrender to the divine within, sinking into the state of restful awareness. We listen to the Voice: *Come this way. Rest in me.* Agitation ceases, emotions steady.

We do not understand how un-restful we are until we experience divine rest. Much of the way we live does violence to the spirit, because it demands things that our true self has no intention of doing. We labor to fulfill obligations. But by being "useless" on the world's terms, we can live honorably and uphold our deepest commitments.

You will find peace of heart when you realize that the Divine is already working in you, calling you to solitude. This is passive contemplation and divine rest, and the essence of the call to love.

February 6

Liberation from False Desires

We are in bondage to material things that we believe are important, necessary, and give life meaning. We are in bondage to an idea of what we have to do, be, and perform, and what the spiritual life is supposed to consist of. The desert monastics called these worldly illusions "demons," the shadow side of personality, where we are trapped by subservience and subjugation to temporal desires. These cultural demands are inferior to the luminosity of being that is already within us. Every day we trade the glorious for the mundane.

To achieve freedom requires a continual reaffirmation of our sacred existence in the midst of all that denies its validity. And certainly there are many things that refute the dignity of life. Yet, if we succumb to this kind of thinking—the demons of despair—then we have given up on life. But despair is also the collapse of the self, and the destruction of hope. This is how we lose freedom. The freedom of being cannot be achieved in one lifetime because it is infinite. Thus we work to eradicate the little demons of despair that constantly tug at faith. That is the goal of our effort: to be free to love God.

February 7

Wild Places

We all find ways to preserve the right to be alone. The use of the word "right" is intentional, because solitude of self is a spiritual right, on the same level as other universal rights.

Perhaps as a child you learned to distance yourself from anything that was violating body or spirit. You found ways to stabilize your emotions by separating from family dynamics. Or, you escaped false silence, the silence that is deafening by what it is not saying, by what it refuses to say.

The Indigenous peoples who revere the Earth and honor the spirit of place interconnect with the sacred bonds of silence. And the American naturalists—John Muir, Aldo Leopold, and others—who advocated for the preservation of vast tracts of pristine land bestowed upon us the priceless gift of solitude.

They understood that wilderness is necessary for the human soul, and if wild places are not preserved, our humanity is impaired and Earth's sovereignty overrun. They wisely intuited that all living beings require spaces of pure emptiness, untainted by human activity or development.

February 8

The New Monk and the Divine Feminine

THE PRACTICE OF a new monastic spirituality is founded on the nondual consciousness of the Divine Feminine. This may be, in fact, its most distinguishing feature: that the Divine Feminine is not solely an aspect of monastic spirituality, the Divine Mother to whom monks pray, or the archetype of the feminine aspect of personality. Rather, this is a monastic sensibility born within and through the Divine Feminine that is bringing into the world a way of being faithful to that Faith which is beyond religion, and a contemplative heart open to the majesty and tragedy of life.

It is a reconfiguration of the human soul on a subtle level, which is so profound and elusive that the agent of that reconfiguration is glimpsed only by her traces. It means redefining personhood not as fallen or wandering, but as the self who carries the seed consciousness of transformation and future renewal. It is to change the focus of humanity's progression in history from deficit to surplus, from deficiency to strength. This is the vital shift in consciousness needed to build a more holy and peaceful Earth community.

February 9

A Weapon of Omission

THE FALSE SELF is a weapon employed to keep people away from your tender heart; it is a weapon of omission, which prevents you from removing the masks of personality. In order for divine love to flow into the soul, the mechanisms of defense that deflect from your tender, sacred being must be dismantled. There is no mystery to the world's violence—it comes from within us. Only real vulnerability makes it impossible to do harm, because in the holy light, harm does not exist. Surrender, vulnerability, is your jewel, inheritance, and success.

February 10

Never Close the Door on the World

WE MUST ASK: Is the history of theology, and by extension, the history of the self, coincident with the conditions of the world?

The rapture of the world is shattering; it calls us up again to the sensitivity of relations, to the irreducibility of historical events, and to the mystery hidden in every particular. We are called to this bearing of divinity because of humility, and because of the vastness of what can never be named, known, or totalized; we are called because of the nothingness that underlies every something.

Although we may try to close our hearts, such attempts only make us less human. In order to keep our hearts open we have to hold the exquisite beauty as well as the suffering and disgrace; we have to expose ourselves to the vulnerability that rests as a root condition; and we have to learn to honor this openness of heart. God does not withdraw.

February 11

Love for All Creation

Compassion is a whole and persistent way of interpreting and responding to the world. It is empathy for and identity with a world filled with discord and lack of faith. Compassionate care focuses on its beloved everywhere, which is an unself-interested love for all creation. The heart that trembles before suffering becomes the vantage point from which we offer acts of compassion to all beings and events. We pray to cultivate the qualities of compassion that foster harmony on Earth, opening our hearts to respond from the perspective of the most Holy.

February 12

HEART OF SILENCE

WE ARE BORN with a heart of silence, nurtured by the vast cosmic solitude. The language of the gods, silence speaks without sound and teaches without word. In the depth of each being, silence connects, sustains, and imbues all things with its holy spark. Children of its mother womb, the entire creation intones the eternal language. No matter how far we stray or how long we live, we are never separate from our source: Silence.

February 13

NEVER AT THE EXPENSE OF DIFFERENCE

TRUE UNITY AND true communion are never at the expense of difference. Every religion is sustained by a vision of oneness at its core. Every religious tradition brings to the heart of the faithful a unique and stunning vision of ultimate reality. The very existence of these religious lineages is sacred. Mystical unity does not reduce a religion's difference but empowers and fulfills its coming to wholeness in the mind or soul of the individual. When we enter a religion in its depth, when we become one with its wisdom, then we know that it is both uniquely true and the source that points beyond itself to greater and ever more incomprehensible mysteries.

February 14

An Organic Constellation of Wisdom

THE COMMITMENT TO seek the ultimate—Great Spirit, Brahman, Allah, God, etc.—is imprinted in the heart of the world. We live in an era of new visions of the sacred and types of religious expression; the monastic heart resides within all people, regardless of life situation or vocation; and it is a sacred duty to share contemporary spiritual ways of being in a world often lacking healthy models of faith.

Whether or not you belong to a religion, or are uninterested in religion, there is a divine path interior to your being, an organic constellation of wisdom imprinted into your soul. If you have the courage to advance into the mystery of your own solitude, you will discover it for yourself. Composed of its eternal nature, you cannot be lost, abandoned, or forgotten. In the secret teachings of love you will be guided on a spiritual journey that forges a path of holiness in your being and in the world.

February 15

A Sacred Attitude of Heart

A NEW REVELATION or universal story is necessary to guide our world today, one that respects the biodiversity of life, tapestry of human cultures, and wide expanse of the cosmos. We need to imagine our world in its sacred and prophetic dimensions; in the promise of all religions and spiritual traditions, and in the dignity of all species and life forms. We need to recover the ancient vision of wholeness and closeness to nature that sustained countless generations, and at the same time broaden and deepen this vision beyond local, tribal, or national boundaries to include the whole Earth community. What we need is a sacred attitude of heart, and a global spiritual perspective that informs our quest for peace and is a fulfillment of the promise of faith.

February 16

Our Life as Prayer

At the core of our collective journey is a vow. When we place Divine Mystery at the center of our hearts, then we truly are living a religious consciousness, whether or not we belong to a named religion. When we place the earthly realm and its entire human and more-than-human inhabitants on an altar of devotion and consecrate our lives each day to their benefit, then we are living a true path—a personal, organic spiritual path. When our daily life becomes a prayer, then we are a prayer of love and healing for the world.

February 17

No Longer Yearning for What We are Not

The condition of mysticism will never be over, for we are of it. We never feel at home elsewhere, but only in the serenity and comfort of our communion with God. We may attempt to make excuses for this state, hoping that it would finally go away and we would then be able to function well in the "real" world. Yet, not only has this never been meant to be, we must no longer yearn for what we are not.

Many of you have expressed a longing for mystical union, for the touch of the Divine, and have suffered over the lack of cultural and religious support, at times feeling lost and purposeless. Yet turmoil is a positive sign that your soul is being stirred by a deep desire. For the mystical path of the heart requires a reevaluation of time-honored religious beliefs, and the openness to emerging revelations. It is the process whereby the soul serves as a birthplace of a universal path of spirit, and a new light of peace toward all beings.

February 18

Now Is Our Time

Our hearts are called to the quiet desert, a desert that looks a bit different today than it did to our fore-bearers, a desert that is so difficult to inhabit with any regularity amid the noise of daily life.

This movement into the desert is not a journey, actually, not a striking out to foreign shores or starry heavens, although these too have their place. Rather the radical wisdom that is the mark of solitary places is discovered when we sink down into the place we inhabit. Through accepting responsibility for our embodiment, and for the ordinary events that give life meaning, we glimpse the habitation of the sacred within our midst. And somehow, in the throes of everything else, comes a spiritual belonging that feels at home everywhere but resides nowhere.

It is almost like saying that, if we were to achieve the enlightenment or salvation prescribed by all our religions —rather than living in some realm after death, in some heaven away from home—we would come back to *this world* ready to work together in the essential wisdom that underlies every religious sentiment: *Let it be on earth as it is in heaven.*

February 19

The Mother Seed (1)

Divine Sophia is the mother seed from which sacred consciousness grows, and the starting point for a global spirituality. This is because in the hiddenness of the Divine Feminine is the principle behind every principle, the root consciousness that incarnates in various forms.

When you experience nondual intimacy beyond religious identity, then everything is holy. Everything is as it should be. Everything is the source of further illumination. You enter into the heart of truth, before it takes on a particular uniqueness. You discover the path of emptiness and the dwelling place of the Divine Mother. When you find Her source, you understand all spiritual traditions and essences, and you sit at the lotus juncture, a recipient of new revelation.

February 20

The Mother Seed (2)

IN THE MOTHER seed we live the formless form, the wayless way that is capable of bearing ambiguity, uncertainty, paradox, and plural realities. Through this mother consciousness, which endures all things, we glimpse the Divine that is always within and with us, is always on our side and supporting us, is always present to us. As well, it is never against us and it never withdraws.

Follow the simple beauty of Her path, and the quiet way in which She enters your heart. She is calling you! Sink into the silky gentleness She brings—like the gray down of a morning dove—and you will be enwrapped in folds of love, your whole being at peace.

February 21

The Truth of Our Hearts

TRUTH IS BEYOND our senses, yet its laws can be discerned, experimented with, and relied upon. Blind obedience is not the way of truth. While truth is unceasing and unchanging, it is not pursued or claimed without critical reflection. Each individual through personal experimentation must discover truth within. Since the totality of truth is beyond our human capacity to know, we can only approximate its vastness. It is an experiment of our hearts, and the challenge to practice the truth of our hearts. Only when we give our whole selves—body, mind, soul, and spirit—to the search for truth, will we begin to understand. If you seek truth partially, you will discover only a part of what you seek. If you seek truth fully, you will enter a new world of meaning and love.

February 22

The Mysticism of Light

We are the mysticism of light in form. We are tangible expressions of intangible wholeness and oneness. The divine light is shining in our souls and in our bodies right now, illuminating us, drawing us to the source. Every word we speak, every breath we take, every touch, every sound we hear, is a manifestation of the divine energies in our mind, body, spirit, and soul. If we do not feel this divine energy, it is because we are habituated to another vibration of consciousness that has wounded us, that has brought us toward a type of amnesia or ignorance in our minds. Nonetheless, this divine permutation is present within.

February 23

The Universal Force of Love

THE UNIVERSAL FORCE of love moves in the direction of freedom. Divine love, loves us in freedom, and is our greatest liberation. Divine love, loves without possession or demand. Therefore, Divine love never asks us to sacrifice the true self to be loved, or for the sake of love. Love can never be possessed.

Over the course of our lives, how often have we given away our true selves in order to belong to the crowd? How much of our freedom have we given away in order to be loved? God's love is not that kind of love. Like Divine love, our love also has to be free, without sacrificing our spiritual need. It never opposes or diminishes the practical realities of life—getting a job, finding a place to live, taking care of children, or sustaining one's self physically.

February 24

Communion with the Universe of Energies

The conversion of life that identifies and stabilizes all seekers of truth is dependent on a restoration of our inherent multisensory, mystical sensitivity. In fact, the person's call to contemplative life is wholly based on a deep spiritual aspiration that by definition cannot be fulfilled by the things of the world. This means that a significant element of the new seeker's formative path requires a recovery of our natural and intrinsic capacity to read the unseen—that is, to enter into communion with the universe of energies.

February 25

The Balance Between Body, Mind, and Spirit

One of the more challenging aspects of the mystical life is the relationship between body, mind, and spirit. The body nourishes the mind and the spirit, as the mind and spirit sustain the life force of the body. In a mystical sense, it is imperative that a balance between these three dimensions of life is maintained, keeping in mind that the Divine is not only the source of all, but intimately imbedded in all dimensions of reality. On a practical level, this means that we will never be able to ultimately avoid or deny the spiritual aspect of being. Every human issue has a divine counterpart. God's beginning is in you. Your inner life reverberates in the mystical heart, as your being touches the Divine being. To truly understand, you must experience this fact.

February 26

Reconciling Our Wounds

Even our most personal, wrenching moments are imbedded in and bound by the eternal, the transcendent. This gives us hope that there is something greater and beyond the present. We learn that words never tell the whole story. The anguish and silent cries—even the heights of ecstasy and joy—elude language. We cannot find in speech what we seek. Only by risking our hearts to emptiness—to the fear that there may be no path and no road—do we find what is immeasurable. We share then in the communion of all the saints who walk the earth—the communion of direct experience.

As we open ourselves to our true feelings, we participate in the beginning, in the undefiled state prior to error, sin, and pain. This giving ourselves away is like the passion of a child, of the unhampered pure heart of the person who has no concept that life could be other than holy.

February 27

Our Attachment to Being "Spiritual"

Contemplative practices—if not kept alive and meaningful—can be another form of attachment that impede the journey and obscure the reason we pursue them. Spiritual practices that are imposed by the ego result in discord, because they bury fundamental truths about one's self, and suppress the unpleasant, negative, or unholy things we harbor about ourselves. When we use spiritual practices as an imposition of the will, they do not lead to liberation, but to further imprisonment.

Often we are not aware of how a spiritual practice can reinforce the false self, or how a person can become habituated to an identity or way of being precisely because of her or his dependence on a particular practice. Then the deeper layers of personality that we have denied start rising to the surface, disturbing the wounds that our spiritual practice is keeping in place. If we are attentive, we may discover an entire archeology of un-masked feelings and attributes that were repressed or held back by our attachment to being "spiritual."

February 28/29

Hymn to Holy Sophia

O, Hagia Sophia, Holy Wisdom, everything we are and everything we have, you gave us. The very air we breathe and the eyes with which we see, you fashioned. The mind that draws these words out of silence and etches them into the tablet of time, you made. You surround us with beauty: the light in the trees at dawn, our companions the saguaro, white-tailed doves resting above the roof, quail and rabbit babies, ocotillos and palo verdes. You are the Moon, rising like an orange disk to call us; and the starkness of the desert Sun that burns away the dross of our souls.

SPRING

March 1

Canticle of Peace

When day cedes to night
and creatures large and small
bow their heads in sweet surrender
May my soul rejoice in
Your serene embrace.

When spirit fills with starlight
and dreams of quiet wonder
wrap me in angelic radiance
May my soul delight in
Your eternal tranquility.

When I awake in the silken dawn
awash with the gentle touch of
Your sweet love
May I, Holy One, greet the rising sun
with Blessed Simplicity.

Now, I step into the bustle,
now I pray and work
now I struggle and rejoice,
In all,
You are my Peace.

Amen.

March 2

Guarding the Heart

Elders know that it is not enough to wear a monastic habit, or to sequester with holy books and sacred practices. The commitment to seek truth requires conscious facility with the ordering of the person's life and protecting the integrity of the Divine within. These monastic rules of guarding the heart can be replicated in those living outside a formal monastic setting by developing the skills of energetic discipline and emotional integrity, which require insight into the mystical intuition of visionary worlds that swirl around us in each moment. This is the path to becoming a vibrant, centered person, open to the sacred universe incarnated on Earth.

March 3

A New Expression of Faith

What we've learned over the last century is that our common spirituality—our global spirituality—is forged together by the prayer of love that transcends religions. It is not a reality that is conceived and constructed by the mind, but a state of consciousness we discover is already present by surrendering ourselves to or sinking down into the spiritual core of life. Global spirituality is an affair of the heart that begins deep within one's soul and is the soul's active expression of the unity of creation that sustains diversity and difference rather than marginalizing those differences. Global spirituality is not solely concerned with the coming together of different religions, but with following a divine call to love in a new way, to be holier. It is a sacred experience on the human horizon that is drawing people toward a mystical, rather than religious expression of faith.

March 4

Our Emerging Hearts

An emerging heart means this: The future of life depends on expanding the capacity of the human heart. Our hearts are capable of loving more, giving more, and caring more for the world. Within us remains an untouched well of passion for life in which the Divine wounds us with love, expanding our capacity to feel exponentially. Illuminated in this way, our hearts are enflamed by the longing all around us to make the world a place where love may flourish. We need a heart philosophy and heart politics, and religions that do not just talk love, but actualize it on Earth. An emerging heart also implies that the Divine comes to us out of a hidden depth, an undisclosed dimension. It is a new creation, a new capacity within us. But it is more than that. In the garden of our hearts, the Divine waters the seeds of a new revelation and a new wisdom nowhere abated. Joined with the weaving together of consciousness and cells, our adoration and our longing become an altar upon which the universe breathes its own prayer.

March 5

THE STRENGTH FOR COMMUNION WITH OTHERS

THE MORE WE embrace inner solitude, the more we acquire the strength for communion with others, and the less we are disturbed by the world's noise.

For many people, relationship demands have dominated their entire life. Often marriage or partnership problems—emotional, sexual, and physical—hinge on this issue: a lack of the sense of self, alone. Unconsciously, we crave time apart without the intrusion of other energies. We need permission to love solitude. Most likely we never learned self-love when we needed it. We learned through difficult experience and pain, but no one reminded us, "If you practice inner solitude, your life will be easier and more peaceful."

March 6

ONLY SILENCE

FOR ALL THE diversity of ideas, religions, and practices found in the world's religions, interreligious dialogue revolves around the Great Silence. In silence, there is no religion to divide or segregate. There is not a Buddhist silence or a Christian silence or a Jewish silence. Only silence. In contemplation, we sink into the silent dimension of reality that is the unifying element in a personal encounter with the religious heritage of humankind. Silence illuminates all things, bringing into relief our fears, anxieties, harsh words, and unholy thoughts. It releases the source of our passion to know ultimate things, to be holy.

March 7

The Unity of Creation

The unity of existence binds our bodies and spirits to the entire cosmos. Our inner journey is not ascetic or self-deprecating; in the first instance it is joy, spontaneous eruption of bliss, what we call holiness or sanctification. This is the spark of every being and every consciousness: a spontaneous, intentional joy of being. It is the ultimate, divinity, working itself out in matter. God, or whatever name we assign to Mystery, is fully present in the world. As so many holy teachers have insisted: the Divine dwells in the unity of creation; there is no place empty of the Divine. And because this is so, whenever we give ourselves over to the power of unification and integration, the old confusions, anguishes, and laments are healed or washed away.

March 8

Ask Me to Give Myself Away

"Oh Beauty, how I do adore you! So weary am I and so habituated to the old ways. Grant me the courage to abandon all, to savor your sweet call that fills my whole being with the delicate ardor of love. Call me again and again and I will come. Ask me what you will and I will answer. Give me a task and I will fulfill it. Ask me to go hungry, send me away in thirst, I will not abandon you. It is your will that my love commands. It is your desire that my life is for.

"Show me what you need and I will do it. Show me what you wish and I will find it. Ask me to give myself away and I will lay my heart upon stone tablets for all to tread. For you there is nothing I will not do. You, Beloved, who wants my freedom, who leads me through the valleys of despair to a Light brighter than any sun, you who have given me the gift of Love: what else can I do to show my gratitude?"

March 9

TEND YOUR FLAME

PRAYER, MEDITATION, AND silence heighten your awareness, make you more sensitive, and lead to a more attuned discernment of the heart, showing you where your spiritual life is going. An image that you might be able to use for yourself is that of a flame at the center of your being. As you tend this flame, you are attending to your devotion to your God.

Whenever the world intrudes on the flame or whenever you feel obligated to step out of that space, ask yourself what benefit is this in your life. Is it in fact taking you closer to the Great Spirit or further away?

March 10

Cultivating the Solitude of Self

WE PRACTICE SILENCE. We practice solitude. We practice prayer and meditation, but we also are very aware and discerning. We are not asleep. We are aware of the movement in our spiritual lives.

The solitude of self is a way of preserving that place of holiness in your own being, to be with God's being, the divine being. At the mystical level it is about the deep inner experience of the Divine. On a practical level, solitude of self implies a place of detachment—where we extract ourselves from daily concerns, professional conflicts, and social situations in order to foster and preserve the right to be alone. It's a place where we preserve in our self the dignity of the solitude.

Solitude is risky because it compels you to the depth of your own personhood—to conflicts, attractions, and demands—to discover the soul's burning fire that is not quenched by worldly things. It is to claim the right to stand alone, to be unafraid of others' opinions and desires; to be exempt from having to be special or accepted, known or important.

March 11

The Way of Silence

SILENCE IS DEEPER than prayer. We have a need for pure emptiness. How different this is than false silence, the silence deafened by what is not said, by what is not truthful! It is far grander than a still night lying under a canopy of stars in Mazatlán. Or the solitude found in the Trinity Wilderness, high in the Sierra range camping among black bears. We have had our share of lonely places. This silence pulsates within, a depth not our own that opens out to a boundless expanse of light. Solitude, alone with the Divine in the soul's hermitage, is not segregation, but intertwined with everything.

How small and insignificant is the self in comparison to All That Is!

March 12

Am I a Mystic?

There is a common misunderstanding about mysticism, that it involves some kind of secret knowledge inaccessible to ordinary humans. The paradox of mysticism is that at the same time it is labeled "secret" or "ineffable," the enormity of humanity's spiritual archives attest to the fact that mysticism is not beyond human understanding but is the capacity within each of us to touch and be touched by wonder and awe.

March 13

Reclaiming Your Singular Intention

So much of life—even monastic life in its traditional forms—is the pursuit of an already established theology, pattern of consciousness, spiritual practice, or understanding of ultimacy. From the moment we take our first breath until the moment we pass from this world, someone or something is labeling the self. Spirituality is nothing more than a deconstruction project of continually stripping away unhealthy, false, or degraded identities to encounter the source of life's fullness. We abandon the known for the unknown. It is the work of the spiritual person to maintain nonviolent resistance to these affronts, and to claim the right to an inner life, and to a solitary encounter with one's divine source.

March 14

PASSION IN THE SPIRITUAL QUEST

PERHAPS YOU WONDER, "What draws me closer to the divine heart?"

Essential to the path is passion: the overwhelming necessity to find God, to know the true self. This yearning to know who you are must take precedence over your need to exist, for existence is not life, it is just getting by. But the passionate need to know one's self, the need of oneself is the impetus and first condition of the heart's path. Your pure longing for God is a spark that ignites the sacred flame and opens your heart to the Holy.

Passion is your strength and fortitude, because it is not diverted by voices that warn: "Don't love completely; don't trust." Passion is the lover seeking the beloved. Whatever trials the lover must endure to reach the beloved, he or she willingly undertakes.

March 15

The Inner Flame of Passion

The longing of the heart is so direct that it is your greatest strength. But just as your heart can be wounded, also can your soul's longing. Your passion reaches out, gets diverted, and weakens your inner fire. Once again, your passion gains strength, pursues its goal, and is diverted. But, the flame can never die, nor be destroyed, for always it remains one and united with the Ultimate Source.

To keep the flame burning in your heart you must pray every day to remain in your intention. Remind yourself what is most important: to long for God, for Truth. The reason passionate yearning is so vital, is because it is direct movement from your heart to the heart of the Divine, and nothing can interfere with this pure intention.

March 16

Goodness is the Foundation

GANDHI READ THE *Bhagavad Gita* every day. In this ancient sacred text, he found the path of nonviolence and the way of truth.

Spiritual principles govern the soul, its present and future manifestations, just as physical laws govern the material world. When we follow these principles of truth we move closer to happiness; when we violate them we move away from happiness. Gandhi held that the highest principle is nonviolence born of God's total goodness. Goodness is the foundation of reality; it is the motivating principle of life. *Satyagraha* (soul force) and *ahimsa* (nonharm) are manifestations of ultimate benevolence.

March 17

Becoming Apostles of the Holy

In embracing a spiritual or monastic way of life, we are guided to become pilgrims, disciples, devotees, or apostles of the holy. The attitude of the apostle is testament to a complete turn of heart, in which the seeker is dedicated to that which is eternal—beyond personal success and even life itself, to some unimaginable mystery. Apostles devote themselves to the transcendent—to the Cosmic Mystery. They give up their small will to surrender to and follow the Divine will. They are not concerned with the marks of success they leave, but rather with how to share God's voice and vision in the world.

March 18

The Quest

IN DAILY LIFE we often experience conflicting desires and needs. We may be torn by our social identities: family background, work experience, history of traumas and triumphs, and aspiration for prestige or position. These social identifiers distract the heart and prevent us from concentrating on our most ardent desire. In the contemplative life, we have permission to live in God's time, to rediscover meaning and authenticity, to the search for our true selves.

When we initially consider giving ourselves to the quest, we may find many reasons not to proceed: "How do I put my attention on God when I have family or work commitments, when I have a spouse or a partner?" Tension arises because we may conceive of the Divine as separate from us, or believe that loving God would somehow mean not loving others or would require giving up our will or freedom. We may harbor a fear that our spiritual longing is a ruse, a deception or trick that is working against us. Instead this call is our greatest gift. We don't know what our greatest freedom is because it is so immense, so benevolent we cannot conceive of it.

March 19

A Web of Love

THE ENTIRE MOVEMENT of the solitary life is propelled by acceptance that the Divine is calling you home. Along the way there will be concerns and questions: "Am I making the right choice?" But these questions are not what prevent you from going forward. What prevents you from going forward is the fear that you will be taken to a place that is against you. A transformation of the inner life occurs when you discover the hidden mystery of your own being, and realize that you are being called to what is truly good, to what brings you happiness. Yet we resist it. We don't trust that there is a force in the universe, a seamless web of being that loves and embraces unconditionally.

March 20

Polishing the Conscience of the Soul

Most helpful in your journey is paying constant attention to every aspect of your day. What was drowsy in the heart, or inattentive in the mind now becomes the material source of a heightened sensitivity: "What did John at the grocery store say to make me feel sad?" I woke up this morning in a place of solitude and openness, and now at 2:00 p.m. I feel fragmented and alone. "What happened during the day to change my mood? What is the source of loneliness? Who is the 'I' that is lonely?" When you are mindful of your actions and see awareness as a natural response to the interior life, you polish the conscience of the soul. The light reflected in the mirror of your awakening illuminates all things anew.

March 21

THE ABILITY TO SEE

THE GREAT CHALLENGE of the inner life and a key factor that distinguishes spiritual masters more advanced on the path from beginners is this: the ability to see the core of another's soul with love and compassion—without judgment, condemnation, cruelty, or piousness; to see another person clearly, dispassionately, and fully, through a heart of love.

March 22

HEAR MY PRAYER

HOLY ONE, WHY do people say: you are perfection beyond me, vision too bright for my eyes, nobility too rare for my soul, love too pure to be felt, and knowledge too glorious to be understood? Your immeasurable gift is already stamped in my depth! Even though I fear you are not present, even though I doubt, or have given up hope, your divine spark is eternal in my soul. I long to dissolve my separation: to see with new eyes, to hear with new ears, to feel with a heart burst open in awe!

Hear my prayer: please draw me ever closer to your mysterious intimacy by which and for which I was born. Amen.

March 23

Peace, the Waters of Bliss

DURING A TIME of tragedy, we pray to hear God's message. The divine voice speaks: Peace, Peace, Peace.

The peace of a pure heart, of an intention to non-harm, of the flourishing of life, and a love for the world. A peace that suffers with the least of us, shedding tears of fire for the majesty of creation. A peace that knows no bounds, and recognizes no authority over mercy. A peace of forgiveness for the ways in which we violate the law of love. A peace that is the power of transformation, of healing body, mind, and spirit. A divine peace that folds us in the arms of eternal compassion. Peace, the waters of bliss, washing through our souls, cleansing humanity of its sad history of violence.

March 24

An Intention of Attention

Mindfulness implies seriousness and care in ordering your life according to spiritual principles; and a realization that it is a full-time occupation, not a part-time project that is squeezed into everything else. Rather, spiritual awareness is your work, or vocation: a state of being that occupies the center of your life. This full-time occupation of spiritual growth and mindfulness stabilizes your soul and allows all disparate needs and longings to fall into place more easily, because your life now is focused on the one thing necessary. Order has been established, and the rest of your life can fall into place.

In this first state of mindfulness, attention to emotions, desires, and needs is central. We learn to become attentive to our emotional tone, and to avoid anger and undue passions. We also become aware of how heedless and careless we often are in daily life. Are we inattentive with our prayers? Are we careless with the way we treat people? When we are always rushing around, we do not put proper attention on what we are doing.

March 25

On What is Important

There is nothing more damaging to spiritual growth than the reluctant pilgrim. Mindfulness thrives on attentiveness and concern; it is disturbed by ineptitude, laziness, and apathy. You may experience a kind of internalized inertia or sloppy disregard for what is important to your soul. How often do we say: "I want to meditate today, but I have to go shopping and I have to call this person, and oh gee now it's midnight and I didn't have time to do that all day." When we are reluctant to find the time to be mindful, we are in effect saying that the spiritual practices and personal relationships that give life meaning are unimportant.

March 26

Murmuring

In the "Rule of Life," St. Benedict discusses how destructive the distraction of constant complaining or "murmuring" is, chiding the monks to dispense with constant gossip. Legitimate complaints, which are a necessary and healthy part of community life, are different than harmful murmuring, which is designed to undermine the community or another person's heart. Complaint often is directed toward a perceived or real authority, which can take many guises, from unexamined family dynamics, religious alienation, personal wounding, social injustice, and so forth. To address these issues honestly is vital to health, and essential to the growth of awareness.

March 27

Disturbances

A SERIOUS SPIRITUAL commitment cannot be completely distracted by every little thing—by people who gossip, are angry, or avoid compassion. This does not mean that we remove ourselves in a superior or arrogant manner. Rather, we apply mindfulness to our relations and we ask ourselves whether this relation is, in itself, healthy. The same is true with respect to removing ourselves from distractions. Distractions can be anything—television, movies, phone calls. There is not a right or wrong distraction, only what is a distraction for you. You have to find out what de-centers you or what fragments your inner peace. That is your distraction. That is your disturbance. It is different for each of us. Find out what that is.

March 28

Spiritual Community

Buddha said, "Right association is the precursor of the eightfold path." When we are not around people with whom we can share our spiritual intention, it is hard to maintain focus. There is a sense of aloneness; but being able to share in community is a great blessing. When we have that, we are very enthusiastic, because we know how alone the journey has been. We have gratitude for community, for sharing, however perfect or imperfect it is.

March 29

Prayer and Meditation

Spiritual masters across traditions express the virtue of intensive prayer or meditation practice. They remind us that the most powerful aspect of life—the thing that changes everything—is ceaseless prayer. This is an amazing statement. There is an energetic consequence of prayer and meditation that positively affects body, mind, and spirit.

Of course, not everyone will have a formal practice. Some may prefer walking as a meditation; others find reading a spiritual text or dancing to be a form of prayer. Through whatever means, expressing one's connection to the source of life is healing.

March 30

Spiritual Work

We all wish it were easy, but it takes work, attention, tears, and laughter to grow spiritually. Yet, even the difficult moments are joyful because they help us develop wisdom and strength of spirit that no one can take away. Worldly success cannot match the achievement of spirit. The greatest human award is without power if one has not found the meaning of love and peace. For the most part, the spiritual life is hidden and often the holiest people are unrecognized. Yet, in their depth they have achieved something for God: they are climbing a mountain toward holiness.

March 31

Deep Engagement

Every encounter with every being is a mystery. There's no face like any other face. There's no person's heart like anyone else's heart. Mystagogy is a deep engagement with whatever we encounter—a tree, a teaching, another person—which evokes a poetic expression rather than an explanation. To enter mystery more deeply is to enter it at its point of holiness. When we encounter something and enter it in this way, mystery graces us with understanding.

April 1

May I be Mindful

May my day begin in mindfulness,
    aware of the divine flame within.
May I share love with all whom I meet,
    in gratitude and compassion.

May I open my heart to all who suffer today,
    those I meet and whom I may never meet.
May I understand how suffering wounds
    your tender heart, piercing my humanity
        with grief.

May my being, broken open by the glory
    and suffering of the world, be transformed
        into a wish-fulfilling jewel.

May my heart this day be beautiful,
    Illumined by fire, enlightened by wisdom
        and softened by compassion.

May joy burst forth from my presence,
    like a bouquet of flowers in full bloom!

April 2

True Rest

We celebrate our communion while we contemplate divine goodness, mercy, and love. The active effort that we make toward celebration of the sacred is not a substitute for secular life. It is not an imitation of the spiritual life in the secular life, but rather the deep soul rest that is the purview of the true seeker. We tend to think that this is something we are going to jam into our regular life. We cannot imitate kindness and consideration and continue to be as busy, fragmented, and crazy as we were before. Spirituality is not supposed to be another thing added onto everything else we are doing. Rather, it is a deep desire to find true rest, which is an experience of resting with God. When do we allow our souls to rest in the Divine? Most of us never rest, because our spirits are distracted, divided among too many interior tensions.

April 3

Transformed By an Act of Grace

We tend to think of ourselves as sinful. Why am I not ordered? Why can I not control myself? What is wrong with me? The mystics tell us that this deep level of self-awareness and self-order comes about through an act of grace. Instead of focusing on ourselves and our foibles, and being angry at ourselves because we are not ordered, we can pray for grace. We can meditate on our capacity to be given the gift of fidelity, the gift of not forgetting. Thus, we must learn to practice ceaseless prayer and asking the spirit for help: show me, guide me, empty me. This becomes a giving over of our will instead of a suppression of the will. In this transformed state of consciousness, our infidelity is healed—our unfaithfulness to ourselves and to others is transformed by an act of grace.

April 4

Recognition and Reconciliation

Mystical gentleness engenders in us repentance and compunction—a conscience that realizes all life is holy—and causes us to feel in our whole being how we violate the sacred. It also provides the means to reconcile our heedlessness, the things we do every day where we just lose our minds for a moment, or we are not paying attention. We have to raise our consciousness, but also our conscience—our moral fiber. If we do not understand our moral fiber, we are not going to recognize it in someone else. We cannot guide someone else if we cannot guide ourselves. We cannot help someone to raise their level of moral virtue if we are morally inept, morally inattentive, or shoving our foibles "under the rug."

April 5

If You Seek a Life of Holiness

True change is about the discernment of those inner secret impulses and ideas that we have that may seem innocent to us, or that we may think are innocent, but that in fact are dangers leading us away from our life in God. Transformation is about the diagnosis of self-truth. Have I really put the Divine at the center? What are my motives for doing what I am doing? Are my motives really for the Divine or are they self-aggrandizing?

Mindfulness helps us to recognize the difference between motivations that lead closer to spirit and motivations that lead away from spirit. In the end, mindfulness is a high state of mystical awareness, a sensitive attunement to the gentle mercy and gift of being. It is the inner discipline applied to daily events, which moves the soul closer to the abundant, exuberant, silent, glorious freedom of being fully alive.

April 6

The Prophet Within

All of us have a prophetic voice that effects change in the social and political order because the prophet's words carry the power of its divine source. The prophetic personality yearns to actualize God's message, seeking transformation of self, family, relationship, or society.

The prophetic personality lives not only his or her personal life but also the life of God, hearing God's voice and feeling God's heart. Such a person imparts the Divine pathos or sympathy for our plight, feels anguish for our misdeeds, and brings joy to our hearts. Each person contains the seed consciousness of the prophetic mind and heart. Becoming aware of the prophet within, deepens one's soul and advances one's spiritual life.

April 7

Ode to Creation

In the dappled dawn
when creation breathes a still note
we find you, Majesty

We are your witness
We are your voice in the wilderness
Our feet tread lightly your mother ground

You made us like unto you
bodhicitta, holy spirit, atman, ruah
We are your body born in matter
Gazing upon your own creation in us.

April 8

The Consciousness of Contemplative Life

THE CONTEMPLATIVE LIFE is subtle, nuanced. As humans we charge through life, often unable to see what is right in front of us, and suffer for our inability to detect the disjuncture between a person's godliness and their mortal limitation. The contemplative life is also practical. It is not an idealized life where everything is rosy; everything is beautiful all the time. Rather, it ushers in an awareness of reality, in all of its multiplicity and a piercing discernment—wisdom—to sort through what is appropriate, what is real, what is possible in this time and place. It is a view in and from the whole. It is an open and free consciousness. It is a compassionate consciousness. It is a silent consciousness that sees and knows. It is a very aware, observant, non-judgmental, and discerning consciousness.

April 9

Being a Fool for God

COMPASSIONATE CONSCIOUSNESS CANNOT thrive in a state where we hold onto our beliefs with willful ignorance or become so rigid in our thinking that the subtlety of reality goes unnoticed. Rather, an awareness of empathy for all life is the result of giving one's self away—being a fool for God. Standing on the precipice of our heart's longing and leaping off. Here we learn to live in the place where self-emptying gives rise to new birth, where letting go is liberation. The more we trust our ability to wholly embrace life, the greater is our joy within.

April 10

Seeing the Truth in Everything

To love the Divine Mystery alone is never exclusive, because all life is the Divine imprint. It is always inclusive, an embracement. Living in a state of "awakeness," it is the practice of opening our hearts to love and holding the world and each other in divine embrace. Compassionate awareness is the sight of the Spirit's own eye, looking upon our hurts, worries, and despairs. When we include all creation in our hearts, we unlock the chamber of holy awareness.

We may fear our own divinity because we think we have to abandon everyone and everything and give up our material life. But while loving God alone leads us through the narrow path and into the dark nights and the radical reordering of being, it is not a rejection of ordinary existence. Rather, love uplifts everything and offers everything over to fullness and fruition. Not an abandonment or betrayal of materiality, loving the Divine Mystery means seeing the truth in everything.

April 11

Loving God Alone

Loving God alone means seeing compassion in everything and having compassion for everything and striving for the integrity of everything—not as an absolute state, but as a process of perfectibility, of wholeness. Seeing God alone means that although we recognize our flaws, sins, fragmentations, broken bodies, broken spirits, willfulness, despair, doubt, anger, apathy, ruthlessness, we do not stop there. We keep the relative in its relative state of consciousness. We keep the truth in its true state of consciousness and we recognize the difference. This does not mean that we will never experience despair or doubt or loneliness or anger. It does not mean that we may not react to other people in their despair, doubt, loneliness, and anger. But it means that we can remember to recognize the difference between ephemeral and eternal truths. That is what seeing God in everything is: loving God alone, love of God alone.

April 12

An Intention of Heart

The Divine communicates in the hidden sanctuary of your soul, and the contemplative is one who desires to keep open this communion.

Contemplation is then an intention of heart—a heart that longs to be ever receptive to God within—and not merely a state of meditative awareness. The Divine never closes the door. God's communion with the soul is constant, even though in certain aspects of the journey we may feel that the Divine is absent, or we are lost and in the dark. Nonetheless, the divine-human communication is always occurring; it is only when we reject the light that shines in our souls that we close the channel of mystical communion.

April 13

Voluntary Awareness

Voluntary awareness or self-disclosure repairs our hearts by awakening us to the underlying oneness of creation and a new sense of responsibility for the conditions of the world. For good or ill, what we do and bury inside ourselves adds to the collective storehouse of consciousness. Everything good we do expands consciousness, and all the things that we bury cause contraction. By a willingness to look within, we contribute to healing and offer a welcoming heart for the birth of the holy among us.

April 14

For the Divine Alone

A contemplative life is a happy life because one knows what one wants. In our daily life, we often have many different desires—many different needs—many different attachments. These needs keep us distracted and move us in contrary directions. The contemplative life is a life in which one arrives at the one thing necessary. One arrives at the place where one's whole being knows what one needs and wants. That very orientation of focusing or mindfulness becomes the source of great transformation.

April 15

Living a Contemplative Life

CONTEMPLATION IS A commitment to living one's life directed toward the Divine Nature or union with God. It is a universal expression of the communion between the deep self and the divine mystery. A contemplative state of consciousness, or state of being, is present in all spiritual traditions in various garbs and by various names, expressed in sophisticated typologies of mystical states: *samadhi*, *satori*, *nirvana*, infused contemplation, liberation, enlightenment. Contemplation is a longing of the self to experience the Source of all that is. A true contemplative does not view silence and solitude as a deprivation from the world, but rather as nourishment for the soul.

April 16

FULFILLMENT

ONE OF THE most difficult of challenges for a person who pursues contemplation is the disjuncture between a worldly and a spiritual understanding of success. In daily experience, we are trained to seek exterior goods, which can become a source of discontent. For the contemplative person, however, fulfillment comes from growing in the spirit, seeking deeper levels of meaning and love, because it is this that is one's true inheritance.

In this sense the contemplative life is radical because it asks us to question: What is the one thing necessary? What brings true happiness?

April 17

RIDING THE WAVE OF AWE

PRAYER IS EVERYWHERE. And we bring it everywhere with us. It is an energy that flows into and out of our souls with each breath, curling and somersaulting in spirals, until letters settle in our mind, and then, caught up in the torrential waters of spirit soon become a rain of words. We cling to these lofty sounds, riding the wave of awe, straight back into the Divine Heart.

April 18

Transforming the Heart

If you have the strength, courage, and commitment to enter solitude, to confront despair, loneliness, and other devastating emotions, you will come to wisdom and understand the suffering of the world. You will be drawn beyond your loneliness or despair into the loneliness or despair that every human suffers. Through understanding the universality of suffering, the heart grows in compassion and mercy.

This method of spirit is true for every pain, and for all suffering. When you let go of attachment to your suffering and realize that this is how all humankind suffers, you will be awakened to a very high and profound path, and be drawn into the heart of the sacred. Your heart will open to the mystical reality of life. Then instead of suppressing or crushing the heart's vulnerability, you will understand its strength. When you are able to withstand self-sacrifice, which the world considers to be a weakness, you will participate in the divine life, and enter a sanctified place.

April 19

The Strength of Love

Your heart has the capacity to transform suffering, to bring the potential into the actual. Ask yourself what you want to bring into the world. Do you want to contribute to pain and suffering or to gentleness and compassion? Do you want to experience love? Do you want to live differently on Earth? If, in your heart, you truly desire to be holy, then you will be given the strength of love to sustain suffering, and to be transformed by divine light.

April 20

Spiritual Wisdom

Spiritual Wisdom is based on a mystical worldview that affirms that the fundamental state of the soul—and of life—is Divine. That is, the human person's external life—with its many manifestations—is founded on and composed of indivisible, inner qualities or virtues, which include love, mercy, compassion, benevolence, joy, and humility. We can discuss the qualities of love, for example, but we cannot break love down into component parts. Love *is*. The same is true for mercy or joy. How do we dissect joy? It is not divisible, because it is a state of divinity.

April 21

ANNIHILATION OF THE SELF

THE VARIOUS MANIFESTATIONS of the mystical life discussed—longing for God, great determination, detachment, humility, and spiritual love—revolve around what is variously described as the loss or annihilation of the self. A familiar and much discussed topic in the world's mystical traditions, emptiness of self is the premier path to enlightenment, realization, or perfection. Described by many mystics as an ultimate stage of consciousness—even beyond mystical union—annihilation is an experience of complete intimacy and openness, which leads the person to powerful experiences of interdependence and unity with all of life. In a state of absorption or interpenetration with the Divine, the mystic describes the true self as empty, nothing, nondual, or indistinct—the self of intimacy, receptivity, and surrender.

April 22

The Spark of Life

Stop for a moment, take a breath, and contemplate the mystical heart. As you read the following sentences, envision the sanctuary of the heart within you.

HERE IN THE sanctuary, at rest in the Unknown, Love coalesces in divine contemplation and breathes life upon the nothingness. Find the place in your heart where the sacred words reside. Divine Love is the principle that brings formlessness into form, and returns living to dying. Love is the catalyst that ignites the dark light of emancipation. It is the womb of creation and the spark of life.

April 23

The Grandeur

Divine Love and other exalted virtues are living realities imprinted in your higher self. You draw on these elements because you have been created of them. So when you act with humility or compassion, you are being drawn toward the higher principles of which you are composed—the spiritual building blocks of being

That is why the spiritual path is so splendorous. We fail to see the grandeur because we seldom pierce the veil of religious imagery to the real splendor: our lives are an enactment of the Divine. These divine elements come together in specific, unique ways, making each of us a singular configuration of divine possibility.

April 24

Love the World Without Limit

There is much for which we can pray. Let us contemplate our capacity to love the world without limit, remembering to preserve and protect the sacred. Let us not allow the world to dictate our capacity for giving, because such openness is the gift of divine, incomprehensible love within. Let us not let ignorance and pain rob us of our tender longing for God, because if we do, they are taking our heart.

April 25

Inexhaustible Language of Love

LETTER BY LETTER and word by word, one begins to comprehend the vocabulary of Love, and the magnificent, sacred sentences. Each letter, each word, touches the very core of one's existence, resonating into sound and spilling over into form. One speaks, and one begins the journey from darkness into light.

It is within the depths of the dark contemplation that the self comes to know the divinity of its nature.

April 26

The Sacred Sentences

Within your heart is the abode of divinity. Our mission is to articulate and to celebrate the coming of divinity into form. We, as humans, are a microcosm of the absolute. Within each being is a particular spectrum of the absolute, and thus each person is a unique expression of the sacred on Earth. And so we tenuously attempt, however faultily and gropingly, to put together the sacred sentences. This is our work. We are the co-architects of sacred words. Each one of us is a unique configuration of sacred letters and each one of us, in thought, word, and deed, births them into form. This is how and why we each have the capacity to know the Divine and to transform consciousness.

April 27

Your Calling

You are a being that stands at the juncture between time and eternity. You are a prism of the entire spectrum of divine light, a unique expression of the ultimate.

Your life is a mystical unfolding—your existence is an integral part of the Divine's journey from formlessness into form. Your life expresses the immensity. Your capacity to search for truth and be truth is your calling. By entering the abyss of dark contemplation and drawing out the sacred letters, you heal a rift in consciousness.

April 28

The Stage of Un-Knowing

Every spiritual journey follows a pattern of illumination, purification, darkness, and intimacy. At some point along the path, everything you believe to be true will appear useless, empty. This stage of not knowing or unknowing is a mystical precursor of divine intimacy, for darkness is, in fact, everything: It is an emptiness of conceptualization. It is empty in the sense that it cannot be grasped, because it lacks separate identity, it is one. We cannot say what it is, and we cannot say what it is not. Without any sense of duality, it cannot be conceived by the mind. Yet this nothing is everything, it is whole. It is the primordial sea. It is the cosmic essence, so complete in itself, it cannot manifest. It is pure potential, pure wholeness. And thus, to the dualistic mind, it is pure darkness, pure emptiness.

This process of being drawn deeper into darkness has been called "mystical unknowing." The soul encounters a reality that exceeds language, destabilizing the mind and confusing the psyche, to arrive at the highest form of knowing: unknowing. Awed by the grandeur of the Holy, the soul is humbled.

April 29

A Reverse Perspective

THE SPIRITUAL PATH requires a reverse perspective, one that looks at oneself and the world through God's eyes. In other words, it requires a consciousness of humility, of compassion and love that seeks the transformation of whatever is diminished by the world into a higher, more spiritual mode of being. It is to submit oneself to the palace of wisdom and to evaluate one's life and activities from the vantage point of the holy. The process of moving into a divine perspective takes time and grows incrementally in one's consciousness, as the person learns to let go of ego attachments, practice humility and merciful conduct, spend time in prayer, and purify one's heart.

April 30

Action From Nonaction

Contemplation builds an inner hermitage in the person's core—a holy respite free from everyday antics and daily distractions—where one does not flee from the world but rather finds it anew. As a return to the center point of love, contemplation touches an inexhaustible ocean of compassion from which all external works of mercy are generated. Fruitful action—action that does not create harm, violence, or pain—arises from nonaction, from a person's capacity to be free from self-interested gain.

May 1

The Earth Turned into Gold

"Praised be You, My Lord, with all your creatures."

In the love "Canticle of Brother Sun," the mystic mind of St. Francis of Assisi writes out of divinity, seeing it everywhere. This world is God's world, the Earth turned into pure gold. Separation is our illusion; it is our willful ignorance and rejection of the immense beauty that surrounds us. The progress of a soul is not measured in terms of personal freedom but is directed to something immeasurably noble: the bearing of divinity with and for each other. Attuned to the shimmering presence and inexhaustible ocean of peace in creation, our hearts yearn to heal every pain with mercy.

May 2

We Learn Silence

Radical openness is never final or complete; it leads us to silence where the retrieval of new sacred speech may be born. It is a necessary element in a theology which, in prayerful and humble patience, waits to receive a salvation that applies to us all. This global theology refuses to segregate and intimidate the "nonbelievers." It is willing to wait—forever if it must—for us (as one interrelated sacred body) to bear the divinity of the world.

How does one remain loyal to this as-yet-unfolding potential? A global theology works toward inclusion and oneness, at the same time that it directs us toward a vision of salvation for the whole. We learn Silence. Confronted with the choice of which path is the more righteous and authentic, we remain sober in orientation: no one path can effect this global awareness alone. We wait. Progress is measured in small increments. Without demanding immediate goals, this theology that is built on the dignity of all creation must be patient. We cannot impose criteria for the journey. It is an arduous pilgrimage, because it has neither been imagined nor achieved before.

May 3

Reverence for Monotony

An effort toward mindfulness is making provisions for solitude and for silence—to be disengaged from the demands of the world, and to practice a kind of creative monotony. For monastics, praying seven times a day, chanting the liturgy of the hours, or practicing zazen can become monotonous. And yet, in the most peaceful of monks is a kind of reverence for monotony, even when they have heard, for example, a particular scripture passage hundreds of times over the years. As contemporary people, we do not like monotony. We like diversity. We like a million possibilities, a million distractions, but to recite a passage from scripture or to sit in quiet contemplation or to be struck by rapt attention affects the physiology of the body, mind, and spirit. Such attentiveness has a beauty to it that affects a tangible fragrance in the soul, when one's day is ordered toward true happiness, and not transient happiness.

May 4

Happiness

NO DOUBT YOU are aware of the difference between the happiness that comes from doing what is spiritually right, versus from the material happiness you get when you buy or accomplish something. These are different levels of happiness. Discernment is all about distinguishing the difference between deep interior happiness and material or superficial happiness. We are so habituated to seeking material happiness that we often dismiss or reject spiritual happiness. It is offered and we reject it. It is available to practice in the simplest and most humble ways, and we dismiss it. To find true happiness takes the courage of allowing the Divine to show us the way. It requires that we relinquish transient forms of happiness in order to discover a deeper freedom that only Spirit can reveal.

May 5

The World of Matter

The world of matter is divine. There is something inexplicably mysterious about the subatomic realms, the universe of cells, and the wholeness and complexity of the body. The physical universe vibrates in multiple states and dimensions of oneness. The mind may distort the unity, consciousness may perceive dualistically, but our bodies exist in an interdependent homeostasis, or we would not even be able to breathe. The physical world is awe-inspiring.

May 6

FAITHFUL TO LOVE

JUST AS WE realize that the spirit offers a different kind of happiness than that provided by the accumulation of material things, similarly we recognize that the love we have for the Divine may be different than what we think love is or should be. When we discover our love for the Divine, then we realize the potentiality for love in all our relations, and in all of life's moments. Mindfulness becomes then an intense longing to be faithful to the love that has been given as a gift and an unceasing adoration of the Divine heart that lifts everyday activities up to their incandescence.

May 7

Discipline

Mindfulness is the ordering of our lives according to what we know to be true. There is a wonderful passage in the Book of Sirach (6:18–20, 26–28) that describes discipline as the mother of all virtues. When we are disciplined, that is the order of the universe. The passage from Sirach refers to an interior discipline, not the discipline that is harsh and imposed from outside, but the spiritual discipline that is in line with the life of the divine. Nature is disciplined. Trees, for example, do not pull up their roots declaring, "I don't want to be a tree!" This may seem silly and ridiculous, but in a way you can see the discipline of nature. The tree practices stability. The tree is a practice of stability. It is rooted in a particular place for the duration of its existence as a tree. So the tree is actively practicing stability. It is also practicing unconditional receptivity because it is taking in whatever comes to it: sun, rain, insects that bore holes in its bark, birds that make nests in its branches. In the book of nature, we encounter the ordering of the mind of God. We as human beings have the free will to be disordered, but the degree of our order and discipline is part of our participation in the divine nature. The act of ordering is important.

May 8

A Rule of Living Conduct (1)

Over the years, I have composed and followed a personal rule of life. I include below excerpts from the original and longer rule, which you may find helpful in writing and living your own code of conduct. (*Provided for the next three days.*)

- Be faithful to the Divine in all that you do. Put the Divine will before your own. Ask, "What would God do ?" and wait for the answer. Do not allow personal attraction or gain to cloud decision-making, or your soul's intentions to be compromised.

- Be simple of purpose. The basis of simplicity is centering on God. The heart of the monastic life is to live in God's presence.

- Love all of creation with Divine compassion. Total commitment brings change. Give to life your unparalleled commitment, and complete love, one that is without self-interest.

May 9

A Rule of Living Conduct (2)

- Offer yourself as a place of prayer. May your presence be one that heals divisions and expands hearts.

- Be attuned to the splendor of creation, and the gentle web of existence. Celebrate embodiment. Actively work—both within yourself and in the world—to make the holy manifest.

- Refrain from possession. Remember the transient nature of earthly life. Possession can occur on all levels: physical, emotional, psychic, spiritual. Love expands the spirit, possession contracts it.

May 10

A Rule of Living Conduct (3)

- Pray daily to grow in humility. Offer over to the Divine your regrets, sorrows, doubts, motives, and unresolved desires.

- In all you do, practice nonharm. Make a small footprint, tread lightly, become aware of the impact your actions have on others. The refusal to reflect on your motives leads to suffering (for others and also one's self).

- Treat all religions and spiritual paths with honor and respect. Enter silence. Keep faith alive.

- Create community wherever you are. Make of your heart a home for the homeless, a refuge for the poor. Pray for the well-being of your monastic sisters and brothers.

May 11

There are no Absolutes

Emptying the self is not easy. You have to pull up the roots of craving, of ignorance, of false attachments. It means being really honest with oneself, being honest with one's true nature. It means being willing to go through the fear that you do not have a true nature, the fear that you are nothing, worthless, and that there is no wellspring, no river of unity underlying everything. The only remedy for this is to practice—to keep leaping off the cliff, divesting yourself of platitudes and conventional notions—to keep moving in faith, even when you cannot see or do not believe. For there are no absolutes in the spiritual life in the sense that we imagine: of having arrived, finally having achieved the ultimate. We discover instead that there are degrees and progressions of letting go. There are states where we come to the end of the long, dark tunnel of self-centeredness and we are filled with the fragrant mystery. Yet even in these states there is always more.

May 12

The Perspective of the Whole

Nonviolence is a state of consciousness that sees reality from the perspective of the whole. It recognizes that oneness underlies diversity and searches for ways to protect the unity of life in the concrete situations of every day. When the web of union is disturbed, our hearts overflow with concern and grief. At the same time, there is a spiritual power of the soul that transforms despair into hope and oppression into liberation. It is because the Divine is infinite oneness that we are touched by compassion and are compelled to rectify through nonviolent acts of resistance the cruelty, insensitivity, and injustice inflicted on our brothers and sisters, and to translate this into a desire to alleviate our suffering world.

This ability to empathize with another sentient life rests on a mystical capacity to identify with the suffering of others and to find in that suffering an expression of a higher truth. So powerful is this truth—that all life is one—that we must always seek it through struggle and persistent effort. To know the world as the Divine knows us is to risk losing the illusion of a separated and independent self.

May 13

A Heart Ever Receptive to God

A GOOD PHILOSOPHY to hold and live is this: every one of our painful or self-destructive emotions and behaviors is built on top of a fundamental wound that distorts the intimacy of divine love. If you are willing to look within, the Divine will guide you through darkness and into your true goodness. The gift of truth continues to surface throughout our lives, despite denials, calling us toward wholeness and healing,

The universal force of love never abandons us.

May 14

MERCY

ACCORDING TO THE great Sufi mystic-poet Jalal al-Din Rumi, it is in mercy that God bears human affliction and it is in mercy that God reveals the vulnerable heart of reality. Mercy is not the attribute of an apathetic, unfeeling God. Rather mercy flows out of a divine intimacy with, and longing for, creation. In human affliction, in the weeping of the outcast and oppressed, in the sorrow of war and pestilence, God mourns with us. While God's severity is meted out in the drama of many religious stories, God's mercy often remains hidden and obscure. Having born the openness of divine intimacy, mystics replicate in language the loss of self that alone is capable of penetrating into God's infinite compassion. Mercy is the fuel that animates mystical language, exposing the vulnerability of the flesh and the inadequacy of absolute constructions. Is at the point where truth lays itself open and bare, without theological justification or ground, that divine mercy is presenced in the bewildered language of the heart.

May 15

There Are No Names

The challenge for the contemplative person resides in his or her ability to be groundless, to be poor of "self." Much of monastic practice is about protecting one's right to be free from another's identity or persuasion. It is the right to be "one's own person." But, to achieve the freedom of the true self, you have to continually be alert to becoming "something." This requires continual sacrifice, emptiness. Otherwise, you become "teacher" or "guru," or "great author." In the openness of divine love, there are no names.

May 16

Prayer in Each Act

THE LANGUAGE OF prayer, which is often desiccated in contemporary culture, yearns for resuscitation, to become again the speech from within. Prayer is not merely linguistic or intellectual but is a living river of devotion bringing divine energies into the world. All forms of speech and types of action have the potential to be a prayer. A Hassidic story asks, "How does one study with a Rebbe?" Well, you watch him tie his shoes. Because if he is a true Rebbe—a true master—then there is going to be some form of prayer in his tying of shoes. In each act, however small, is prayer.

May 17

The Arduous Journey

ALL AUTHENTIC SPIRITUALITY is hard won, involving a decontructive process that leads to fundamental changes in one's psyche, heart, and soul. Taking apart the belief in a separate self, contemplation is profoundly dynamic, embodied, and interrelated with the whole complex that makes up the person—mind, body, soul, and spirit. As it leads to a deeper and more fundamental change of heart, the mystical encounter exposes our wounds, suffering, oppression, doubt, and fear. It is an arduous journey, and requires that we get to the root of the meanings, structures, and social constructions of daily life. It is radical as well because contemplation demands a certain kind of honesty and a certain pure intention that clears away the debris of the mind and the sloth of the heart.

May 18

Mysticism and Feminism

The dialogic relationship between mysticism and feminism implies that the study of mysticism cannot remain abstract but is compelled to address its cultural, social, religious, and spiritual dimensions. As lived experience, contemplation is not free of the gender bias, clerical exclusion, and theological subordination of women in patriarchal cultures. Similarly, the goal of feminism—the dignity of women—cannot be waged in isolation from the deep mystical and contemplative dimensions of women's struggle. Feminism is inseparably related to the transformation of the whole interpretive framework of unjust and sinful relations that women use to construct meaning in their lives. The categories of consciousness that surround and confine the spiritual life of women are embedded in and tainted by dominant religious norms.

May 19

Co-Liberating God into the World

GOD CANNOT CREATE or lead the soul to the true reality that has been there all along but must suffer and wait for human cooperation—until we love ourselves with such an intensity of love that we break through inferiority and self-doubt. Then, the divine being is manifested in our being, co-liberating God into the world. God is curtailed by our oppression, just as God is freed by our dignity and empowerment.

May 20

The Journey of Self-Healing

Those of you who have been pursuing a spiritual path know that your body and spirit demand change. It becomes intolerable to continue to abuse the true self and to deny the soul's desire.

The journey of self-healing, the path of the heart, requires that you pursue the dark night of faith, without knowing where you are going or if you will arrive. This journey requires that you develop spiritual strength, resisting the pull of the "real" world of spiritual limitation. Only you can affirm, "I seek the Beloved, and I am not settling for anything less. I don't care who ridicules me; I am going to find the true self."

May 21

The Soul's Capacity for Emptiness

Because of the soul's capacity for emptiness, we learn there is no final revelation and no ultimate name. We cannot be confined by a single theological system because revelation is always moving beyond its self-definition. We can only be aware of the vastness in which truth emerges and seek to make meaning in the partiality of our limited grasp of divinity. For in this movement is the foundation of the soul's liberation and a method and means of salvation. A deeper level of spiritual growth occurs when the soul learns to bear the detachment of the mystical desert beyond religious forms.

May 22

Heart of Solitude

THE MONASTIC HEART astonishes us. It is the fountain of silence that relinquishes our attachments. It is the inner hermitage of solitude that rests on three spiritual vows: dedication to the divine within; commitment to inner transformation; and prayer, the life of adoration. An intense desire for union with divine life seizes the monk's will and becomes the compass of his or her entire being. This essential first step is the fuel that ignites the fire of the soul and provides the inner strength to pursue the arduous path.

May 23

INTEGRATING THE INNER AND OUTER LIFE

THIS DISSOLUTION OF the soul into the ocean of divinity begins the process of integrating the inner and outer life. All that we long for, all that requires healing, all that yearns for wholeness, is resolved in the Divine Wound of Love. Not by austerity, not by repression, not by coercion, not by sacraments, not by liturgy, or erudition, but only by becoming vulnerable to God. As the Divine shares all of our troubles, cares, pains, and triumphs, we share in divine gifts and bear God's suffering for the world. There is mutuality and reciprocity, and it is that desire to be a disciple of holy intimacy that literally changes our life.

May 24

Women's Divine Humanity

WOMEN'S FACES ARE undeniably windows into the sacred; they call forth an obligation and a mystery that only can be grasped in all their excessive, yet simple, grace. This claim of women's divinity initiates the mending between sacred and profane—that binary opposition that underlies Western patriarchies and keeps our world bound in chains, offering homage to an antiquated and punishing narrative of sin. External agents cannot impose women's claim of bodily integrity, a sacredness of self that cannot be scape-goated, pushed down, or defiled. It is a spiritual intention that must grow inside the soul of women.

May 25

Emptying of Self

THE NAME OF God is always pointing toward an internalized emptying of self, a passion to be open to the cosmos, to the future, and to the freedom from knowing "I exist." As we swim in the ocean of formlessness, enlightenment is just another way of saying, *true feeling*, *true dying*, *true loving*.

Whether the mystic discovers a personal or impersonal reality, the deep self is flooded with a benevolent and a loving power, such that the heart is torn or wounded by an immense yearning nowhere assuaged. Having experienced alienation and aloneness, the mystic in us feels this aching benevolence and sweet tenderness of God and suffers over their absence and loss.

May 26

Releasing Prayer

Releasing prayer is important. Prayer is not an ideal outside the self; nor is it one more obligation that must be added to the pile of commitments already on your calendar. Prayer is released, uncovered, from within. Each person, when given time for silence, or the peace of a retreat, at some point finds prayer spontaneously flowing from the heart. The release may happen immediately or it can take weeks, but prayer will overflow, whether it is heartfelt thanks for the day, an expression of wonder at a sunset, or long-held grief.

May 27

Embraced by Mercy

Whenever we turn away from our depth and wisdom, we diminish our spiritual potential. We become *less* than we *already are*. When we cease to deny the inner voice, and cease to believe that what is outside is superior, we find that Holy Sophia has always been with us. When we shed our inadequacy and our fear, we touch the source of blessedness. We experience the emptiness from which all religions grow and the mother seed that is the progenitor of the universal call to contemplation. Through mother consciousness, bearer of all things, we are embraced by Mercy, which is always for us, never against us.

May 28

The Real

CONTEMPLATION ILLUMINATES THE real behind appearances, concentrating one's whole being on the permanence that fuels impermanence, the love that is greater than division and fear, the inseparable goodness and holiness of self, and the crushing experience of interdependence that forever rids one of the illusion of a separated self-willed identity. Those who have discovered its living way no longer mistake the constructed for the real, and thus rightfully have rejected the imposition of any theological authority that controls or dictates one's relationship with the Divine.

May 29

The Unimaginable

Mystical texts refer to the immediacy of divine presence, witnessing to those moments when we are not in control of reality and the unimaginable breaks into our awareness, flooding our whole being with insight. It is our capacity for realization and not just knowledge, when we come face-to-face with reality and not just representations. Like a painting or a poem, mysticism reveals what *is* in a new way. By igniting the generosity and intimacy dormant in us, mysticism enflames the heart with compassion for the world. Caught up in a devotion to the divine other, mysticism traces a potential intrinsic to the better part of human nature—what we call the saintly or holy, the enlightened or realized.

May 30

None are Exluded

During the midnight grace of the soul's transformation, when stars stand still and stones are soft, we are given an injunction: Do not privilege one religion over another. The claim of absolute truth or exclusive salvation violates the secret teachings of love, tearing a hole in the fabric of creation and wounding the universal heart. Here is something else astir in that command: The unimaginable and universal mercy of God is not to exclude anyone, believer or unbeliever. So powerful is this commandment that we are vowed to uphold it. The Divine not only is the source of religious diversity and dialogue, the foundation of nonviolence and peace, the fount of benevolence and mercy, but God also suffers—with us and for us—our possessive and narrow hearts.

May 31

Tenderness Beyond Comprehension

ALL LIFE IS pregnant with intimacy. We swim in the cosmic amniotic sea; we are connected through an umbilicus to Source, to Mystery that never withdraws. Bending down to embrace our broken, swollen hearts, Divine Mercy leads us to a palace of forgiveness. Holy Benevolence quickens us from within, enticing us to shed ancient stories of retribution, fear, and sin. An inescapable cosmic unity invades stars and heavens, subatomic realms, and every living form. "God" was the name we applied to an intimacy and tenderness beyond comprehension, to a divine bearing of creation in all its beauty, messiness, and glory.

SUMMER

June 1

Our Radiant Earth

May we find in our hearts the inner cloister where You,
Divine Mystery,
arrive in the night without sound.

You draw us into the beauty and pageantry of your Solitude.

You show us how to manifest your Light
in the soul of the world.

You grace us with the gift of Humility,
becoming vulnerable to Love.

May we protect and sustain your Holy Presence
in all our relations,
on our radiant Earth.

Amen.

June 2

The Heart's Way

THIS IS PRECISELY the path: follow the heart's way and you will be guided. Because the mystical heart is an organ of perception, and a force of light that cuts through illusion; it is a longing in which "like seeks like"—the commonality of divine love in each thing. Just as in this moment, the energy of these words are reaching out to your heart: "like seeking like." This movement of the heart is totally neutral, without will or intent. The heart seeks to know for love's sake alone, without judgment.

Like the physical heart regulates the circulatory system and cardiac output by rhythmically contracting and relaxing, the mystical heart, the seat of the Divine, pulses through the energetic pathways of spiritual consciousness and into the finely tuned atmosphere of soul and body. Vestiges of the mystical principle of love are imprinted into spiritual and physical matter, from the smallest atomic particle to the grand cosmic expanse. It is this high mystical principle that seeks expression in daily life and that sustains the holiness of creation in its various manifestations.

June 3

The Eternal Path

THE CONTEMPLATIVE JOURNEY is an interior and organic process of spiritual growth, encoded in bio-spiritual pathways of the deep self. Activated by the soul's longing for its Creator, each path is forged in the context of life experience, and thus each is unique. At the same time, all true seekers join in the universal path of spirit. Anywhere in the world, at any time in history, when people have sought the Divine, they have traveled the eternal path. It is said, as well, that the heart longs for God with such intensity because God has longed for it first.

June 4

We are a Microcosm

Ibn al-'Arabi, one of the most influential Sufi mystics in Islamic history, says the way to knowing our oneness with God is by praying to rediscover one's passion for the Divine, because it is the hidden key, the secret mystery that will break apart the illusion of separation. At the highest levels of spiritual passion we become concentrated into a spiritual power that gathers together all of the planes of being, all of the divine names so that we experience for an instant that we are a microcosm of the Absolute. By the passion of our beings, the love of our beings, we have the capacity to experience all that is—the comprehensiveness of all that is—all that we are, all that the Divine is.

June 5

To Be This

THE WHOLE TRAJECTORY of Christian mysticism is to encourage us, to inspire us, to impassion us to long for intimacy, to long for this union for which we were made. And when we think of the mystics, we tend to think of them as abstract people, these great beings that we could never totally identify with. But, in actual fact, when you really get inside their lives, you discover that they lived very ordinary lives as well as extraordinary lives and what propelled their lives was this intense desire to be in union with God. It was not an intellectual pursuit; it was the whole passion of their beings—to be this, to participate in the divine life.

This idea of union is to make us understand that our lives are holy, that we can sanctify our lives and that every day we live is an inscribing of divinity in the world. If God has been made human, it is so that humans can be made God.

June 6

Awaken Us

we throw ourselves upon Mercy
in the fiery openness of Divine Heart
    giving up our limitations,
    our possessions, our inadequacies
remind us of the vast multitude of creation that
    groans beneath the thinnest veil of pleasure
remind us of the hungry cries of those abandoned
    by the cruelty of our world
attune us to the voices of the oppressed
    the silent masses of
        humanity
    our earthly kin
        rocks
        trees
        oceans
        dolphins
        owls
awaken us, O Holy One, to the wellspring of Love.

June 7

Intimate Unity

"What is mysticism?" While there are varied definitions, perhaps the most consistent definition is that mysticism refers to a person who has had a direct and immediate experience of the divine presence. And the mystic is a person who doesn't just know about this reality, but who has struggled toward intimate unity with it, so it's not just a one-time experience, but has transformed one's whole being in longing to be like God. It is an embodied process of self-transformation to probe beneath the façade of daily life, to uncover the true hidden meaning and purpose of existence—Who are we? Who are we in the eyes of Love? What are we doing here? That is the mystic quest.

June 8

The Empty Soul

THE MYSTICAL JOURNEY leads to freedom in the soul, a freedom to live as our own beings without the weight of historical traditions or other people's opinions pressing on us. When we break through established modes of theology and behavior, something in the soul is released, and we glimpse what it means to live free and unencumbered. We become adept at spiritually dying, no longer afraid to just let go, let be, and let God be. We can really just cross over and break through. To be this free in oneself is divine.

It leads to strength of soul, a spiritual resilience that refuses to be oppressed or pushed down. This strength of soul develops from a great determination to follow the path no matter what obstacles one finds on the way, for love of the holy. We discover a deeper poverty and a deeper detachment from name, identity, and accomplishment. It frees us to experience a detachment that brings us closer to God, because the empty soul must be filled by God.

June 9

To Live Another Way

ANOTHER FRUIT OF the seeker's path is the ability to remember joy in the midst of sorrow, peace in the midst of turmoil. It is a balancing of the truth of the world and the truth of inner unity. We still understand that the world is fractured and pained but in the midst of that we also know that the Divine Unity is calling us continually to see another way, to be another way, and to live another way. The great strength of the spiritual life is to recognize that we can bear divinity in the world, now. Every attempt we make and strength we develop to work through our pain—and every moment of love and kindness—helps others in some way. This efficacy of spiritual presence is enhanced by emptiness of self. The seeker's heart turns its attention to everything it sees because everything it sees is a reflection of Spirit in the world.

June 10

The Arms of the Unknown

THE LONGING TO experience truth gives us the courage to claim dignity and equality with God. It gives us the courage to shout out, "Yes, this is what my life is about and this is the life of all of us!"

To live without a "why"—living life in the present moment, letting go of the need to achieve results from our prayers or prestige from our acts—is to realize that we throw ourselves into the arms of the unknown, and take the courage to seek this eternal place, without knowing at the outset where we will end up. Once we have experienced this, everything we do, every breath we take, every act we perform, and every moment of life is sacred.

June 11

The Way that is Within Us

IT IS NOT the method we pursue, the stages of the spiritual journey, whether we are in a dark night or illumined, or whether we're beginners or we're advanced—this is not important. What is important is the sincerity of the quest and the longing to know God. The lives of the great mystics demonstrate that it is the pure heart that longs for love, and the humble heart that seeks without self-interest, which draws Love to work in us and to bestow blessing. No one can give you the path to self-wisdom, because it is within you. The way of love is interior, so interior to your being that until you come upon it and until it works itself through you, you don't have a home, really. It is this "Way" that is within each of us.

June 12

A Deeper Solitude

IN THE *Living Flame of Love*, John of the Cross describes how the restlessness in our souls represents our unfulfilled longing, because we know we can go deeper, we know we haven't given all.

In contemplation Spirit teaches us very quietly, very secretly, without us knowing how, without the sound of words, without the help of any bodily or spiritual faculties. As we move deeper into silence, at times the consolations and the joy found in prayer are taken away. We are being drawn to a deeper solitude that is beyond all of our faculties: both the sensory faculties of sight, hearing, taste, and so forth, as well as the spiritual faculties of memory, intellect, and will. And in this dark passage, silence overcomes our attractions and identities to bring us to a love that only can be experienced by self-surrender, by letting go.

Through love, fear, anguish, happiness, and pain, through life's challenges and joys, the soul yearns to draw closer to its Divine Source. Until we are able to open our hearts to love, our souls will be restless, longing to experience divine intimacy.

June 13

The Great Doubt

The whole of the mystical life is an affirmative process of transforming the old self, and growing closer to the Divine self within. But, it is also a journey of negation, where we dismantle falsehood, cynicism, and denial, and confront our fears that God is not truly one with us, in order to realize the blessing of being created in the Divine image.

This is the freedom that cannot be taken away, the freedom of letting go of everything that is less than God. For the contemplative process of affirmation and negation is necessary to combat the soul's greatest difficulty: truly believing that we are divinely beloved, that we are worthy of this love, and that this love is for the sake of our freedom.

The pain and suffering that we go through is because in the depth of our beings we cannot believe or imagine that this is true. So the dark night, the great doubt, and other types of purgative transformation, are in great measure not only about purging the sins we commit, but also, and even greater, about healing the anguish and disbelief that we could be loved in this way. The dark night is that "glad night—that night more lovely than dawn," as John of the Cross says, because even though it is painful it is where we come back to our original nature: lover and beloved reunited.

June 14

One and Simple

The Divine and eternal Presence and the inseparable unity of the Divine in the soul are not metaphorical statements, but are facts of our nature—who we are and and how we are made. We are created with closeness to Holy Wisdom. In the depth of our souls there is a spark, a place where She dwells that touches neither time nor space. This inner spark is completely one and simple, as Wisdom is one and simple.

June 15

If We Could But Glimpse

Because our souls always are in touch with divine love within, when we do not feel or remember our origins we suffer the internal division. If we could but glimpse the luminescent beauty of a soul, we would realize the profound majesty and goodness that created us, and devote ourselves to healing whatever stands in the way of the sacred presence in our lives.

In a sense, we could say that the whole journey of a spiritual life is to realize the special goodness and splendor of the soul always united with its creator. It is the process of moving from outer, affective prayer into deeper dimensions of contemplative prayer that lead us to mend the divisions and restore our original faith.

June 16

Creating a Welcoming Space

If we refuse to violate the code of humility and mercy, if we refuse to cause suffering to others through religious exclusion or domination or superiority, we will find the mystical desert where all our religions meet, and the mystical heart that draws us to love.

Given the inequalities in our world today and the ways those inequalities are created and sustained by structures of economic, political, and military power, the mystic in us must be committed to creating an environment in which those who are historically left out of the conversation feel welcomed and unthreatened to speak at the table of belonging.

June 17

Mystical Solidarity

THE MYSTIC UNDERSTANDS that part of our job as humans is to bring forth and lift up the divine spark in each thing. We are called to actualize divine concern in our everyday relations through our commitment to bringing the voices absent from the conversation to speech—those voices that are voiceless because of death, persistent hunger, or systematic distortion of their lives. We are challenged to work together to bring the Spirit's gifts of unity and reconciliation to building a sacred and beloved community on Earth. We are challenged to mend the rift between rich and poor, spirit and body, injustice and compassion, and to work toward the alleviation of ecological degradation, violence, war, and moral temerity.

We are called to mystical solidarity with the entire Earth community, striving to be votaries of peace. We are called to bear witness to the great benefit that the mystical life affords us at this time in history.

June 18

Communion That Surpasses Words

One of the highest aspects of the spiritual life arises from an existential fact: the greater the quieting of the ego self, the more we are open to universal divine consciousness.

Those who follow the monastic way realize that humility is the great equalizer and the bitter medicine necessary to draw out the sweetness of our beings. For the vow of the monk, and by extension the unspoken oath of every sentient being, is to be for others, to be universal, and not solely for the self. In this way we come to love each other. When we let go of our egos, we let go of the superiority and hidden violence we harbor toward the other. This is how we know truth intimately: when there is no division or separateness.

June 19

The Paradox of Being with God

IT IS QUITE a paradox to be fully open and fully loving and yet fully alone; the paradox of being with God in our daily lives. Some call this inner solitude detachment, some call it emptiness, and some call it annihilation. But the name doesn't matter. The only thing of vital importance is that daily we practice being radically open and radically in love with the world, at the same time that we center our hearts on the Divine. For it is precisely this centering that gives us the strength and courage to devote our lives to the holy, without distraction.

June 20

Our Inner Monastary

WE CAN SAY that every one of us contains within an inner monastery or an inner hermitage where we are alone with our Beloved. No one is allowed to disturb this primary relationship, this bond of intimacy that makes all other intimacies what they are and long to become. So vital is this solitude to our full presence in the world that the attainment of inner quiet is critical on every spiritual path. Yet, for most of us, we are defined as a self for others, distracted by the numerous roles we perform, the many commitments imposed, and the demands internalized. To find the monastery within is to discover the place of rest from which all other relations flourish and grow, and to bask in the palace of inner quiet claiming our right to be alone.

Solitude is solace and silence is food necessary for the nourishment of the whole person and the actualization of our deepest possibility. Here, silence washes away the harsh and violent words that humiliate and shame. Silence is a balm that assuages whatever falsely names or blames. It flows out of untarnished Beauty into the beauty of the face, and into the mystery of being. When we dwell in silence other people are drawn to rest in the eternal presence.

In the inner monastery we celebrate our unnaming in order to be renamed as Beloved.

June 21

This is Healing

Some things in life cannot be bought or taught. They cannot be bartered but only given. They cannot be learned but only born. They cannot be known but only endured. They cannot be named but only lived. This is healing. While it does not succumb to the marketplace, its mysterious ways can be invoked, like the flautist tantalizing the cobra in the marketplace, or the shaman calling the rains. If we enter in mystery, mystery may presence itself. If we open our hearts, pouring everything out, love may enter. If we honor the intimacy, splendor may overcome our hearts. In this way we may approach the awesome truth. We may humble ourselves to learn from that which transcends all learning. We may discover a new way of heart.

June 22

The Impulse of Each Breath

Here is the precious gift of contemplative solitude: we discover in the hidden mystery of our own being that we are being drawn by divine love to what is truly good for us, what is best for us. And we resist. We don't trust that there actually is a force in the universe, a seamless web of being that loves us unconditionally. This lack of trust and its attendant fear fracture the heart's pure intention, generating an inner dividedness that makes what is most natural appear difficult or impossible.

But, when in confusion or fear meditate on this: the impulse of each breath is toward the Holy. First and foremost the heart of every person is seized by a longing for God.

June 23

THE MEETING PLACE AMONG RELIGIONS

ROOTED IN CONTEMPLATION and techniques of spiritual enlightenment—prayer, meditation, and self-sacrifice—global spirituality moves out of silence into a deep engagement with and appreciation for the other. Through silence the meeting place or convergence among religions is found; for in this pure openness we are capable of healing differences and holding multiple religious expressions in a unified whole.

June 24

Global Spirituality as a Lived Practice

ON A PRACTICAL level, global spirituality asks us to consider: How can the spiritual disciplines I practice, and the value I derive from my personal relationship with the Divine be of assistance in mitigating the suffering and ills of the world? How can the wisdom of other traditions enrich my own religion's beliefs and practices and assist me in overcoming elements that are harmful or oppressive to others? On a personal level, a global spiritual perspective calls us to a greater compassion and to practice the spiritual virtues of love of one's neighbors, altruism, and devotion extolled in the world's scriptures. It is a lived spiritual practice that confronts the assumptions of individualism and self-motivation that permeate our culture today.

June 25

A Journey of Openness

This journey of openness to other religions or to a spiritual life without religion is born of prayers and tears. It is not a superficial entertainment or a naïve belief. Rather, it is a wounding felt deep within the self that calls into question and suffers over the violence of exclusion, indifference, superiority, injustice, and oppression—subtle and overt—that inhabits religions and turns the heart against itself.

Thus global spirituality is not a personal construction but an inflow from the Divine, a revealing of a new way of being religious. It is a faith experience, a call to become more loving, to become more holy.

June 26

Honoring the Sacred

A globally sensitive spirituality practices heart consciousness by uniting in oneself the false distinction between holiness and materiality. The heart sees the entire creation in all its manifestations as subjects; therefore all things in the world, all human and more-than-human life forms have inherent dignity and worth. The mission of a spirituality of wholeness is to expand the individual kernel of a religious orientation to include the social, collective, and cosmic. It labors to make actual the highest states of spiritual wisdom and thereby transform the consciousness of the planet through recognizing the crucial role humans play in honoring the sacred presence on Earth.

June 27

The Spirituality of Our Future

Our work is to mine from the oppressions and violence of the world the invisible sustenance of love and humility that lead us to the promise of the Beloved Community. This transfiguration of self and society occurs through activism and interiority. It may be manifested through works of social good and through the inner life of prayer. Whether active or interior, socially engaged or in meditative states, the spirituality of our future requires a contemplative attitude, one grounded in silence and solitude.

June 28

NEW EXPRESSIONS OF THE SACRED

IN THE LIVES of contemporary seekers, there is a desire for a spirituality that is not austere and ascetic, but is directed toward flourishing of life and peace on Earth. We seek a spiritual worldview that embraces our humanness, rather than denies our bodies, and further unites mind and heart, reason and intuition, male and female. New faith experiences are initiating people in a spirituality that is not divisive, exclusionary, or superior, and a vision of truth that is not absolute, dogmatic, or punishing, but one which celebrates the unity and interdependence of all life forms, elevates female and male to their highest spiritual capacity and recognizes our daily struggles to be more compassionate, generous, and caring. One that affirms and encourages new expressions of the sacred.

June 29

A Different Orientation

A QUESTION FREQUENTLY posed is whether there exists a genuine spiritual foundation and sacred path for people who identify themselves as multi-religious, spiritual but not religious, nonbelievers, lapsed or dissatisfied members of their denomination, or simply seekers of a new way.

In some primary sense, these questions arise out of an old paradigm, a collective consciousness formed by the history of discrete religious identities, tribal affiliations, and formal declarations of truth. The answers we seek require a different orientation to the inner life and to the subject of spirituality. In order to understand the future born among us, we need to dispense with the belief that authentic faith is already determined and has a name. We need to recognize with humility that we do not know nor can we control how divine love takes root in a person's heart.

June 30

A More Profound Unity

THE QUESTION OF interspiritual or interfaith dialogue raises deep spiritual issues in terms of what it means to be a person of faith and a spiritual seeker of enlightenment or salvation. For, historically, the spiritual journey has been expressed in terms of specific religious traditions and communities.

Interspiritual, interfaith dialogue at the deepest level implies a different orientation to the spiritual life that is radically nonviolent. It raises issues about truth and ultimate reality, about the very foundation of who we are and who we hope to be. Perhaps more importantly, it asks us to question the exclusiveness of religious belief that judges "outsiders" and segregates them from the circle of love.

Each one of us who yearns for peace must search within to uncover the tendency to reject or diminish the dearly held belief of another person's religion. Until we can discover a more profound unity in our hearts, we won't understand what it means to live a truly spiritual and non-violent life in the world today.

July 1

The Mystery of Your Call

THE JOURNEY TO the inner world is singular—meaning that no one outside yourself knows the mystery of how you are being called. And so it is very easy for others to judge, to question, to wonder…why are you doing this? Are you antisocial, do you not love your family or your community? But the rhythm of the inner life, of God's life in you, is not the rhythm of consensual life and the singularity of the journey is part of the courage it takes to live in the monastic heart. We each have to struggle toward finding the singular path. Therefore we have to be willing to withstand the criticisms and confusions that come our way.

July 2

Inner Intimacy

Essential to travel along the divine road is the formation of a monastic heart. This invisible intimacy between the Divine and the soul is the center from which all action forms. For our inner monastery creates a window that opens in two directions. Daily we pass from solitude into the world, and from the world into solitude. Out of the communion of silence comes community. Out of the aloneness of silence comes relationship.

July 3

Betrothed to Silence

We all contain, to a greater or lesser degree, a monastic personality. Those who have awakened to their contemplative nature, whether they self-identify as extroverted, introverted, intuitive, and so forth, share a common temperament: an intrinsic need for silence and solitude.

This type of person does not thrive in an environment that runs counter to the interior call, but only thrives in the quiet and aloneness that is nourishment for the soul. The food of silence is so vital that without it, the soul suffers impoverishment.

The monastic personality ultimately discovers that regardless of one's personal attachments—single or married, with partners or children and so forth—one's ultimate commitment is to the Divine within. This realization—of being betrothed to silence—changes one's life orientation. In silence everything and every love is included; nothing is excluded as one becomes centered in The Center.

July 4

Silence is Vital

Silence and solitude are necessary for the mature spiritual life. They prevent distractions from entering the tabernacle of the heart, healing the harsh words and noise of everyday experience. We know silence is vital because in our inner monastery, alone with God, all transformation occurs. Here the desert father Ammonas, a disciple of St. Anthony, says, "Behold, my beloved, I have shown you the power of silence, how thoroughly it heals and how fully pleasing it is to God. Wherefore I have written to you to show yourselves strong in this work you have undertaken, so that you may know that it is by silence that the saints grew, that it was because of silence that the power of God dwelt in them and because of silence that the mysteries of God were known to them."

July 5

What All Persons "Ought to Be"

In *The Brothers Karamazov*, Father Zossima says that a monk is not a special sort of person, but only what all persons "ought to be." The monk symbolizes one dimension of our natures and the possibility that each of us can reach this dimension. Although not everyone is suited to formal monastic life, we all have a contemplative dimension that is worthy of cultivation. The challenge of being modern, uncloaked monks consists in the attempt to integrate what every person "ought to be" into the wider social and personal circle of our lives. As we enter the archives of monastic history, we discover how these ancient resources can assist us in integrating all aspects of contemporary life—work, family, friendship, and sexuality—into the sacred dimension of being.

July 6

In Praise and Thanksgiving

Let's a take a moment to
    sanctify this beautiful day.
This day that asks nothing of us
    and provides us with its grace.
Let us in our hearts offer ourselves today
    to the alleviation of suffering in the world,
    that our commitment and devotion
        will be a benefit to all beings.
May we together, in our love of the Divine
    find the strength to seek truth in
        everything we do.

July 7

Listening

Cooperating with grace means that we seek divine guidance, we open ourselves to answers from the spirit realm, from wise elders, and from the study of scripture and spiritual texts. We maintain a posture of openness and humility, listening for the tender, quiet, and often shy voice guiding us from within. To follow the Divine will and not one's own will. To listen deeply and obey the wisdom learned by asking the Divine within.

July 8

Transformation of Love

How joyous and how glorious it is to be called by Spirit! How amazing and how mysterious, just to be called, just to be asked, "Come with me." For isn't that what the Divine has asked of each of you? To be present, "Here I am," to be healed of the distractions and the wounds, to simply accept that the call has been in your heart all along. To no longer turn away, avert the face, or refuse to believe that the transformation of love is taking place in your soul. To follow the call in unknowing, blindly at times, in pain and sorrow, in illumination and hope, determined without understanding, seeking without knowing what is sought, and having faith in the light when there is no light: this is following the call.

July 9

May Our Lives be an Offering

LET US BE grateful for the call, for the preciousness of this life, for the intelligence and health of our spirits and bodies, for traveling the path of the mystics and saints, for being shown a new way, for seeking the Mystery that can never be contained. Let us be grateful. Let us remember as we go about our day, that we are called by Holy Wisdom! How amazing! How joyous! How mysterious! May we be blessed; may all creation be blessed. May our lives be an offering, in our own small way, to the restoration of our beloved Earth, and to the renewal of the world's heart.

July 10

A Model of Loving Concern

By extending the role of the karmic yogi to the transformation of social and political conscience, Mahatma Gandhi embodied a unique expression of monasticism in history. His life vows were directed to every area of endeavor. He was interested in diet, illness, and health. He ministered to people in the ashram like a nurse, proficient in applying bandages and studying Ayurvedic medicine. He was deeply concerned with women's oppression in India, and the plight of children.

But, perhaps the center to each of Gandhi's vows was the complete surrender of the heart to God. Monasticism was an opportunity for intense spiritual development, a model of loving concern for the turbulent world, and for pursuit of total, inner transformation. It was purity of heart, an undivided heart longing for God alone, that he sought.

July 11

We Are Each the Mystic

From ageless time, humans have sought, through direct understanding to know whether there is god or truth or any meaning in life. Seekers are never content to accept the status quo or to believe what their religions tell them without questioning, without finding their own path to the ultimate. This search and its effect are mysticism. And it is the mystical quest that underlies and informs global spirituality today.

July 12

The Mystic In Us

WHEN THE BOTTOM of the soul has dropped away and the self is free to be no-self, we enter a realm of consciousness and sphere of activity that moves out of a subjectless state. It is the silence within us that is older and prior to religion and deeper than the unconscious. This mystical dimension is, thus, not a rarified spiritual state but a further depth dimension within all human awareness, operating alongside other ways of knowing, including the rational, intellectual, and aesthetic. The mystic in us is the knower of the unknown, see-er of the unseen, who is able to withstand—without sacrificing or abandoning love—the contradictions and confusions of the world.

July 13

Archaeology of Our Souls

Spirituality is an infinite progression into the heart of joy. Unfortunately, one of the most basic misconceptions about the spiritual journey is that it is unattainable, and that it maintains a distinct identity separate from the one who seeks. Nothing could be further from the truth. Rather, we are patterned of it. We excavate its unique character through the archaeology of our souls. Thus, the spiritual path is the medium through which we personally unravel the hidden workings of the universe. The spiritual path is one that cannot be learned about. It can only be experienced.

July 14

The Nature of Joy

Three elements are consistent within the spiritual journey: it is a life of which we are composed, its heart is spiritual joy, and it is impossible to not attain one's true self.

Certainly, the ego may impede progress or deny it altogether. The mind may resist, citing that such a feat is unattainable. Fear may intrude, as well as social customs and religious doctrine which restrict one's progress. Yet, despite all resistances, the spiritual path will erupt within us. It must, of it we are composed. No sin is too great, no error too grievous to prevent our highest destiny.

This is the nature of joy: we are founded in divinity, and we can attain nothing less than that, no matter how long it takes.

July 15

Offering Our Lives In Service

Today we are challenged more than ever before to work together toward building Martin Luther King's "beloved community." Through the witness and lives of modern saints, we learn to direct our efforts in service of societal reform and devote our time to the unification of differences.

In response to global tragedies, these women and men of faith offered their lives in service of refugees, to those who suffer from racial injustice, soldiers in war, starving families, survivors of genocide, and other members of the human family whose dignity is debased by calculated violence or indifference. They practiced a circle of compassion that included everyone and excluded no one or no thing, all the while retaining the humility, insight, and sacrifice that hollows out one's soul and prepares it as a vessel of the Divine. In their own struggle to come to terms with the anguish and violence of their day, they forged a path to the mountaintop, to the dream of what is to come. They could see it, and the seeing commanded a practicing of what they saw. There was nothing left for them to do but to embody the coming unity, the unity of all the differences in oneself.

July 16

Longing to Live Another Way

During a conference on world spirituality several hundred representatives from the world's faith traditions were in attendance. Hindu sannyasins were seated next to Thai Buddhist monks; the Orthodox prelate shared a pew with the rabbi from Russia. Zen monks, Zoroastrian priests, Hopi elders, and Jain mystics offered prayers in one voice.

It showed how tangible and real is peace. The experience was symbolic of how community rises out of contemplation and how great shifts in human planetary history begin with the actions of a small group of individuals longing to live another way. There was a desire to love differently, to practice what their hearts felt, as if what they felt was too large for the kind of love they were told was enough. In the presence of our swaying, rocking congregation, there was an expansion of souls. As participants pressed up against old biases and ancient enmities palpable in the air, instead of suffocating under the weight of so much history a collective heart was born. Out of an unknown depth, they became co-creators of an emerging global consciousness and a new dream for our Earth.

July 17

Transformation is Our Nature

WE ARE MADE for healing, because we are made in the divine image. We are beings of change. Transformation is part of our natures, intrinsic to matter and consciousness, the journey of the soul to its source.

We are not destined to be perfect—not here, not now, yet neither are we merely flawed. We are beings born to assume suffering in order to stretch ourselves toward the highest expression of conscious love. In this sense, mystical healing attends to the wounds of the deep self, of the ways in which the soul has been separated from its beloved. The healer weaves the patient's suffering into one's own being, until a gauze knits together the place where the patient's soul is torn. And what is that gauze? It is love. It is compassion. It is justice.

Thus, the efficacy of healing depends on a quality of heart rather than on knowledge or technique. Who you are as a person is all-important. You may have knowledge, but if you are not a lover of truth, are not trustworthy, lack ethical standards, and don't have a prayer life, what difference can it make? You will not be able to harness soul force, which requires the cultivation of virtue.

July 18

The Courage of the Monastic Life

The monk's vocation, if you will, is to challenge the prediction that you will never know your true self, and that you always will be separate from your Source. Monasticism—taking of vows, living a rule of life—is radical. It reminds us over and over again that this world is both a veil obscuring and a window into the realm of the holy. For this reason, monastic life requires audacity and courage, and the full surrender of one's heart. It is a way of being that seeks the triumph of freedom.

July 19

The Emptiness of Our Attachments

SOLITUDE IS THE emptiness of our attachments. You hear that so much, "You're attached, let go of it, be detached." But what do these words mean?

What detachment really means is freedom from useless cares and preoccupations, a freedom from all the things we're so sure are important but really aren't. A life of prayer is a life free for love, and that's what matters. In the end, that's all that matters.

July 20

What is Your Way?

We each have to find our own way. What is your way? Here is where we can get trapped in the artifacts of the spiritual life, and it is really tricky because spirituality of whatever religion or stripe has its own rules and regulations. But the externalities of a religious or spiritual worldview may not be your path; your path might even be in protest of traditional forms of contemplative practice. This is where people who have been studying for a long time, who are not novices on the path, get stuck: when the demand of a spiritual teaching or practice becomes its own distraction because it is not leading you to the hoped for solitude and peace.

One way to discern whether your practice is authentic is to be attentive to what distracts and pulls you away from truth. If you are able to identify and remove those demands that take you away from your heart's longing, you will always be following the divine path within you.

July 21

The Heart of Life's Passion

We spend so much of our lives denying—and being trained to deny—that fundamental, intense passion to know and to be known; to love and to be loved. Central to the contemplative life is the desire to give your whole self to something, to finally be completely and fully present. A passion for the Divine is the one essential intention of authentic spirituality. A helpful meditation: *What is preventing me from giving my full self to God, to what I really need and want?* Whatever you fear you will have to give up is nothing compared to the love you will receive. The fears, resistances, or beliefs you harbor that if you give up "x" (whatever x is)—you will be alone, you will be nothing, and your life will be meaningless—are false. Because when you offer the passion of the spirit, you are given gifts far greater than what you fear or seek.

July 22

When The Spark is Ignited

THE DIVINE IS an absolute and total gift. It is outside the economy of debt, outside the economy of karma, or cause and effect. It is pure gift: all forgiving, all giving, all love and loving. If you've never had an experience of such a gift, then that can be your prayer: *Show me how to receive the gift.* Or, if you've never said to yourself, "I'm going to long for truth with every ounce of my being," then that can be your prayer. Because those who have achieved spiritual wisdom are people who felt an intense desire for truth.

It doesn't matter how your passion manifests, what matters is that you discover the depth of longing in your own heart for the Divine. When this spark is ignited, everything in life changes, for you know then that you have touched life's passion for itself.

July 23

Finding the Center

WHAT DOES IT mean to live contemplatively today and how is that possible? It's such a big question for those whose hearts long for God. The suffering and the joys that we go through every day—the contemplative life becomes a way of finding some kind of balance, calm, or joy in the midst of all these diversions, attractions, distractions that pull us away from the center.

Contemplation is finding the center, it is living in the center where the Divine dwells in you. It is a feeling state. If someone were to say, "What does it feel like to be contemplative, what does it feel like to be spiritual in your self?" It feels like being pulled into a center, into something that doesn't let you go. You are literally pulled into your own inner solitude, to such an extent that while outer things in the world may distract you, there is something fundamentally connected. That connection never goes away, it is eternal. It becomes ever more deep, just as the connection with a loved one gets deeper the longer you know them.

July 24

WE LONG TO KNOW

YOU FALL IN love with your child the day he or she is born, but there is a maturing of the connection that goes on through the whole life that cannot be diminished. It's the same with contemplation: you have been seized and called and claimed and attached to your source: God, Silence, Buddha. By whatever name, you've been pulled into something from which you are never free, in the best sense of the word, because it is your home.

Why is this so necessary for us, why do we yearn for inner solitude? Because we long to know the Divine. We long to know what is our true source. Just as the Divine longs to know us. As the Divine longs to find us in our own hearts.

July 25

The Fruit of Our Love

LOVING GOD ALONE is never exclusive. Living in a state of "awakeness," it is the practice of profound and compassionate awareness. It is a commitment to open our hearts to love, and to hold the world and each other in the Divine embrace. It is, in fact, our capacity to love the Divine wholly that is the source of all other loves. Committing to a spiritual life orders our priorities in a different way and allows us to maintain a focus and direction often sadly lacking in relations. We begin to see that compassion, so central to the spiritual life, is the fruit of our love for the Divine. It is the sight of God's own eye, looking upon our hurts, worries, and fears. What would the Divine see or how would the Divine act toward our suffering or the suffering of others? What makes us sing and dance with joy; what brings to others holy grace? This is what loving God alone means.

July 26

God's longing

We love the Divine for its own sake. We do not love God because we seek forgiveness or receive gifts. We do not love God on our own terms and in our own time. We love because love makes us whole, it is all we are, all we wish to be. In love we find Love; we discover the source of Love. God is not the object of our affections, or the answer to our prayers, but the length and breadth of our adoration. All desire is this one desire: to share in God's longing to be known.

July 27

HOLY CLOTH

GOD IS ALL in all. Although we recognize the broken spirits and wounded hopes of our collective body, we long to experience the manifest unity of creation. In fleeting moments we are granted a glimpse of the mysterious oneness that weaves all our relations into holy cloth. As the illusion of our separate existence is dispelled, we are awakened to life's interdependent whole. Our very existence depends on this interlocking web of being, on the sanctified essence brought into form. To surrender to this oneness is to offer ourselves over to the awe.

July 28

Emptiness of Self

We empty ourselves to let the Divine flood us with love. We are empty so we may be full. As the sign of authentic spirituality, this desire of love to be free of self is so common across cultures that it may be considered a primordial dimension of human consciousness. Defined as the releasing of ego attachments, loss of self is a central characteristic of spiritual life. A complex notion, let us refer to the emptying of self in a twofold sense: as a breakdown of our cherished self-identities, wants, demands, and ego struggles; and as an openness of being, where all the doors and windows of the soul are thrown back to allow in the splendor of life. Since in a body we will always have elements of personality traits, self-emptying is not an absolute state but the practice of letting go. And this practice of detachment, in which we experience the fluidity of presence that is deeper than any identity, becomes the medium for the great transformation of being that demarcates a contemplative life.

July 29

The World Without Veils

WITHOUT LOVE OF the Divine Mystery alone, and emptiness of self the contemplative life is without substance. Through attentive love and loss of selfishness, contemplation transforms our quality of life and the way in which we live. It opens us to loving the Divine with all our hearts. It gives us the courage to let go of the ego self and shows us the pathless path that liberates our souls.

Sufi mystic-poet Jalal al-Din Rumi tells us that all love is in fact love for God, since all existence is the Divine reflection. When we love God alone we find in the ordinary events of life something of the miracle and majesty of the divine mystery itself. When we see the world without veils, we finally realize that there is only one object of our desires: to see God face to face in all things.

July 30

Divine Love

THE DEEPER SPIRITUAL life is not something that we "do." It is, in fact, the activity of divine love working in us. This activity is so subtle and mysterious that we often do not recognize it as it is happening and we frequently do not know how to read its signs. Contemplation is initiated by the touch of the Divine, mending the exile and the estrangement of our separateness, and therefore it is both the healing of a deep inner fracture, and the infusion of divine love that cloaks and protects the soul from anything contrary to love.

July 31

Reunited in the Divine Heart

Beginners in the spiritual life are aware of two things. They are aware that they are struggling to mend an inherent divide within themselves, and they are struggling to achieve moments of illumination, truth, and love. Those more advanced in the spiritual life feel the pain of longing to be reunited with the Holy. They feel the pain of no longer living a divided life. They recognize that the more arduous and fruitful path is the one in which we give away our conflicting desires in order to center our whole life in Truth. So the fracture or pain we feel at different levels of the journey whether we are beginners or more advanced has to do with a conscious awareness of our distance from the holy, and a longing to experience intimacy, to be reunited in the divine heart. By resting in silence and solitude, by offering our lives to the divine pursuit, our soul becomes a refuge for the indwelling of love.

August 1

Blessed Simplicity

It is intrinsic to human nature to be better, more holy. To find the deep source of meaning and the quality of being that are essential to live authentically.

The contemplative part of our nature lives in protest to the complexities of life—to its busyness, numerous demands, and disjunctive intentions. Underneath competing desires and attractions, and alongside obligations and responsibilities, the precious realization emerges: the simple necessity for one's God. Our whole being seeks the blessed simplicity of finally having found what we truly want.

August 2

Prayerful Imagination

Spirit speaks through the imaginative, visual, and auditory qualities of your being. When you open yourself to the eye of spirit, you will tap into creative resources that will teach you new things about yourself.

Imagine yourself as a disciple at the feet of a monk or a spiritual figure you admire. In your mind or on paper, draw a visual map of qualities associated with this person's life. Notice the ones to which you are drawn, and those that are repellant or cause fear. Allow yourself time to explore imaginatively the images, emotions, and thoughts that arise.

August 3

Befriending Silence

While most of us will never live in a monastery, we can learn to master the spiritual virtues and the quality of being that flourish in solitude and silence. As we walk through the imaginative doors of the monastery, and figuratively enter the monastic enclosure, we desire to study those spiritual disciplines and ancient structures of consciousness that will deepen our own contemplative practice. Immediately we are struck by the absence of superfluous noise. There arises an intuitive recognition that much unhappiness in life is the result of never hearing one's own silence, or experiencing the freedom of solitude.

We have a rare opportunity to cultivate this monastic dimension outside the monastic enclosure, and even outside a denominational form. For in meditative awareness, or in centering prayer, we find the radical emptiness that is more primordial than religious identity, and more nameless than the qualification of being Christian, Buddhist, Hindu, and so forth. Just as St. Francis gave voice to the mendicant tradition, an innovation in Christian spiritual practice, or Ramanuja pioneered love poetry in twelfth-century India, we are called today to plant the seeds of a new kind of monastic devotion.

August 4

A Period of Silence

CONTEMPLATION IS NOT something we "do." But we can discern some of its signs and foster its growth in our hearts. What is the still voice inside calling you toward? Is there an interior intention for a different quality of being, and for a more simple, holy life? Try to listen to that quiet voice that enters like an old friend coming by for tea. Give yourself time each day for a period of silence. Let the silence fill your being and overflow into your mind and your heart. No matter how little time you have to devote to silence, keep up the practice.

August 5

Divine Self-Emptying

CONTEMPLATION DEMANDS A certain resiliency, a certain honesty of spirit, that no ordinary life can hold. It is not merely a spiritual way of living or a code of conduct, it is God living in us, and uniting us to God's own life and unity. Called to a relationship with the inner life of divinity, we are led beyond our own self, and even beyond God, to participate in Divine self-emptying. Our soul becomes the emptying, and the liberating pouring forth of divinity. We become the source and fount of openness. God is birthed in us.

August 6

Interior Happiness

Happiness is hard to find. Most of us do not know what makes us happy. We are attracted to transient happiness, to those things whose brilliance fades like flowers dried by the sun. Often the things that make us most happy remain unnoticed, or are pushed outside the conscious mind as impractical and unattainable. So confounded are we by what our neighbors, family, and media tell us happiness is, we neglect the deep, inner happiness that is the source of great awareness.

True happiness comes in through the door of our hearts quietly and without fanfare. When we follow this deep happiness, we are filled with an interior rightness that worldly desires cannot convey. We realize that although worldly happiness may appear more glittery and golden it quickly wears off leaving us more despondent than before. Instead, inner happiness comes from Love's secret touching of our souls. As we become aware of the stirrings of the spirit we are able to distinguish true joy from outward attractions that leave us spent.

August 7

In the Desert Silence

In the desert silence, we discover the well from which spiritual traditions spring and the emptiness of heart that contains all religious forms. We stand before religious thought, before the great systems of theology, even before revelation. Each of us, in our emptiness, contains the seed consciousness of all that is.

When we return to the desert and see God face-to-face we realize only unity. We do not know how or why we have been graced with many expressions of faith. We do not understand the differences and conflicts, at times. Yet in our hearts we have the capacity to contain all these divisions; we have the fullness of being, which is always an unbeing, to heal the difference. And we have the strength to not withdraw.

August 8

Women's Mystic Presence

It is clearly understood today that intimate violence has an enormous impact on women's spirits and self-identity. Women who have suffered from intimate violence experience profound soul wounds that often imperil their inner security, propel a crisis of faith, and estrange them from their most significant personal and community relationships.

We cannot assimilate fully the extent of the suffering women experience worldwide. But we can understand that there is a divine concern with the integrity of women and the honoring of the holy in them. As women demand their inherent right to spiritual dignity, they become powerful forces for social transformation. In honoring women's mystic presence, we must do everything possible to refute the death-dealing politics and subjugating cultural norms that contribute to global female violence, and commit our hearts to the flourishing of the Divine Feminine in women and girls.

August 9

Pillars of Love

As one sheds the divisions of the mind and the temptations of the body, one begins to wander amid the pillars of Love.

As one disbands with the ephemeral human response, the way of reaction and fear, the soul instills insight into the heart and directs the action along the course of another way.

To replace fear with love and anger with compassion, one will experience the meaning of wisdom. As each human weakness is eliminated, the language of Love becomes known. For each small sacrifice is sufficient to enable the heart to behold the grace and infinite wisdom of Being.

This is the language of Love, where we learn to speak the simple sentences of wisdom, embrace the divine passion, and rejoin the holy path.

August 10

Divine Namelessness

LIKE ALL PROFOUND and worthy experiences, contemplation is not without its anguish. No one can hope to escape from conflict, ambiguity, and doubt. For our concepts about religion, our holy endeavors, our worn-out words, and our feeble attempts to control our lives will be burned to ashes by the holy flame. This radical questioning and annihilation of our identity even strips away the claim to a final and absolute faith. In the dark luminosity of being, we are torn from the God of culture and tradition to find the Divine Namelessness that is freedom. Then our hearts are capable of withstanding multiple dimensions of the sacred and of rejoicing in the absence of knowing.

Contemplation is the gift of being; it is a gift of joy and humility. It is beauty itself, to live life immersed in the rivers of silence and in the flowing ardent heart of Mercy.

August 11

INTO THE ARMS OF LOVE

ALL IS NOTHING compared to the Love. Prophets and deities, masters and knowledge, holy incantations and profound art, are mere images of All that Is. To cleave unto the mortal, no matter how holy, is to insert external structures between oneself and Truth. For only in complete abandonment of image, in total dismantling of the self, can one experience Mystery directly.

Nothing can be owned in this realm of the sacred. For nothing is needed. In the total abandonment of self-identification, one embraces infinity Itself.

August 12

Abandoned Self

When all is still and night descends upon the soul, the heart yearns for love's serene abandonment. In the darkened, solitary night, where no mortal eye beholds, the worldly shell unravels, exposing layer upon layer of human image. Stepping outside of time, the heart lays down its fears of ultimate nakedness and awaits the holy embrace.

Like useless weapons the human defenses are lain upon the soil of Love, revealing the jewels of vulnerability. Pride, arrogance, and shame rest side by side with fear, anguish, and despair. Jealousy, hate, and ego are melted in the living flame.

Without name, without home, without profession or relation stands the revealed soul, unclothed and blameless in the night. Devoid of thought, idea, or prayer, the heart prepares for its moment of overwhelming Love.

August 13

The Transparency of Self

LANGUAGE IS NOT a constructed intrusion on the face of being; it is the linguistic fabric in which the transparency of self is simultaneously concealed and revealed. Born from the root of emptiness all words are but attempts to grasp the sacrificial nature of divinity—where every disclosure is a participation in the primordial generosity. It is a tangible link to the world of indistinction and a poignant reminder of the tension that exists between silence and speech.

Everyday we sacrifice silence in order to be worded and to bring to word. We wrench from the stillness the mysterious naming that births communication, and we bear this naming for the sake of the unmanifest. Each life each day is a tribute to the ineffable mystery taking form.

August 14

The Eternal Now

CONTEMPLATION IS FALLING into the arms of God. It is intimacy with the Divine, and a sharing in God's inner life. Contemplation is the root dimension of our natures and the deepest possibility of a spiritual life. It is that life that is fully awake and fully aware of the awe and majesty of existence. It is gratitude for the beauty of the world, spontaneous joy in the face of life's uncertainties and pains. It is an experience of the invisible mystery that lends life its vitality and its wholeness.

Contemplation is beyond words and sounds, beyond the mind's need to grasp, beyond religious forms, and even beyond our own self. In these moments of silence and solitude the soul finds nourishment that worldly relationships cannot provide. Contemplation draws us into the mysterious action of the spirit, and bathes us in what Meister Eckhart, the fourteenth-century Christian mystic, called the Eternal Now. In every breath we are called to the divine desert to purify our hidden motives and the hidden doubt that assails our spirits. In a certain sense, to enter into the realm of contemplation we must die to the old self in order that a new self can be born.

August 15

What is the Path?

What is the path? Is it truly a road upon which one steps, moving ever closer to God? Is it a direction, a way one moves from one place to the next? Is it a method or a journey? Are there one or many? What is it?

The mind is fascinated with its own ability to postulate such profound questions. It is not the answers that are important to the mind, for no answers truly are sought. It is the capacity to utilize the mind that captures one's attention.

Without postulating a true question, that is, one which seeks a solution, there can be no answers and one will be left stranded amidst the digressions of the mind. A sincere question, one which captivates one's entire being, will always seek solution. Questions that posit the ultimate meaning of existence, or the intense need for understanding, will be answered on the level they are asked. Some questions are so vast they are not immediately answerable; it may take a lifetime of learning to comprehend the profundity of the solution.

August 16

Mighty River of Compassion

We need a new thinking of the religious and a more radical expression of the mystical that begins from a premise never before considered on a global scale. We need a spirituality profoundly respectful of humanity's diverse participation in the sacred, that is also unifying and humble, rooted in the earth, sustained by the diversity of life forms, and respectful of the emerging wisdom traditions.

We need a shared spiritual vision able to address our universe and humanity's place in it as an integrated whole.

But religious openness does not require us to leave behind our love for our own savior, messiah, bodhisattva, prophet, or god. Rather, we are called to witness the unifying stream that runs like a deep current within each of us, and to harness the power of these streams until a mighty river of compassion floods our world with love.

August 17

Sinking Into the Center Point of Love

Contemplation is most frequently associated with the practice of silent or passive (receptive) prayer. But it also refers to an inner monastic attitude, a centering point of one's whole life and being. This centering reference may be taken in solitude or in the marketplace; but it never leaves the ground of its longing, turning one's whole life toward creation, hope, and love. Further, this living, daily prayer breaks through into one's mind and heart, teaching those insights, wisdoms, and realizations that uplift the soul.

Far from being unfocused, ephemeral, or rare, contemplation and mysticism seed a person's consciousness with the ordinary and tangible presence of mystery in every facet of existence. In a way, contemplation turns the world inside out. It unleashes a distinctive mode of consciousness that is more passive than active, more illuminative than intellective, more merciful than just.

Having opened the vault of a hidden reality, contemplation is the repository of a receptive way of seeing the world with its own set of principles and properties. Agitation, restlessness, and division cease as one sinks into the center point that is love itself.

August 18

STANDING ON THE BORDER

WOMEN TODAY STAND on the borders of a new country, mapmakers of uncharted spiritual territory. It is through them that new visions of the Divine enter our world, and new spiritual pathways organically form. Having been drawn by a force greater than faith to a "place" in their own soul that is beyond the name "woman"—and even beyond religion—women live between realities. Unable to go back to damaged self-images and classical religious views that subordinate them, women are breaking through inherited cultural patterns and religious systems into new revelatory landscapes that transform the whole of life.

For much of recorded human history women have been representative of two poles of a paradox—as temptresses to be feared and suppressed, and as immaculate virgins of divine purity and beauty. In naming and healing this split through the experience of women, we unite an ancient division in intellectual history between body and soul, matter and spirit, human and divine, and humanity and the natural world.

Through the recognition of the soul wounds and contemplative processes that compel women toward liberation, we discover a new integration of male and female that transforms the quality of our humanness and restores the heart of creation.

August 19

Discerning Our Path

In the contemplative traditions, discernment means to sift through and distinguish Spirit's involvement in your life from egoistic desires and inordinate attachments. This movement is experienced as consolation when it is aligned with divine life; and it is felt as desolation when it is dissonant from divine life. This is the discernment of spirits or the discernment of signs that guides you on the contemplative journey.

August 20

The Many-Faceted Levels of Love

Love reveals the reality where no judgment takes hold and showers the aspirant with welcomed respite from human sin. It is the Love which teaches one the Truth of surrender and instills the balm of divine Grace.

Love, then, is the shield and the warrior, and the mighty fortitude which prepares the self to conquer the inner pains. Love strengthens and heals the wounds exposed by life's struggles. And Love serves as the necessary understanding which prepares the heart to witness the soul's many-faceted levels of Love.

August 21

Endowed By Birth

You have been endowed by birth with the universe's longing. You are born with spiritual strength, with the capacity to know the Divine directly. All spiritual traditions speak of this. Sufis say, "God longs to be known." Mystical Judaism says, "The Lord created a space, a nothingness, *ayin*, condensing within and birthing the world." Creation is born from a passion inexpressible in thought or word: the passion of life for itself.

Igniting our longing for the holy begins in us, but fans out into the entire creation. Know this longing. We are composed of it; it is beauty. Viewing creation with divine sight, through the eyes of compassion, renders the soul in awe, and makes it impossible to violate the sacred trust. In this is the answer to peace.

August 22

DIVINE LETTING-BE

THE SIGHT GRANTED in mystical unveiling is one that sees from God's perspective, from the luminous darkness that defies absolute transparency. If in language we find traces of the mystics' encounter with the humility of spiritual poverty and ambiguity, it is in their lives that the most eloquent statements of radical openness, compassion, and love are expressed. The divine letting-be is the fountain from which peace gushes forth; it is in the dying of the false self that the Divine is born anew in this world.

August 23

The Weeping of Fire

SAINT CATHERINE OF Siena writes about the weeping of fire and the tears of fire the Holy Spirit unleashes in our minds. The weeping of fire—what a way to say it, and something only someone who has been there could write—has no tears because it is the blaze of the spirit in us, drawing us to feel our helpless, hopeless attempts to make things "right." We can all go crazy before we admit that we weep—yes we do—because of what we see and feel that breaks our hearts. This is the wound of love that flows through us and suffers in us the penetrating sweetness and unspeakable beauty of the world.

August 24

The Ocean of Intimacy

The force of the mystical in us compels the heart toward mercy and alleviation of injustice. The whole of the mystic temperament is caught in the pathos of the world and is never free of it, even—and perhaps more so—when the divine wounds our hearts with love. The moments of heightened awareness or the touches of divine love come freely, attuning our hearts in the process to the precious gift of life and to the striking pain of so much of humanity. We are never outside the circle of the Divine, but always swimming in the ocean of intimacy within the joys and sorrows of existence.

August 25

CONCEALED WITHIN LIFE ITSELF

IT IS NOT that this reality is not religious or against religion; it is just that the "religious" is already contained within it; there is no need to demarcate its presence. The sacred does not need grand adornments to dress it up or formal gowns to make it palatable. It is already and always more than we can possibly bear and far more than we can imagine. Further, there are some of us who are hermits and wanderers, who feel most comfortable in silence, on the edge, without a religious home. We cannot have a God with a name. For every name would be somehow blasphemy; and even though we honor names—Jesus, Buddha, Mohammad, Moses, Krishna, Woyengi, Corn Woman, Goddess Durga, Great Spirit—we are called to claim none as our own. This is our faith. This is our calling from that mysterious oneness concealed within life itself. This is our secret. But it is an open secret that cannot be contained.

August 26

The Way of the Heart

The Way of the heart is premised on the assumption that there is something to Know. That is, that something Universal exists which transcends history and in which one can find answers to the multitude of questions locked within human existence itself. This methodology does not say, however, what will be known, whether what is known has a purpose or a meaning, whether the nature of the known is good or bad, finite or infinite. The Way of the heart does not impose judgments nor predetermined conclusions. It simply seeks to Know, with all its being, with all its love.

Paradoxically, what the heart seeks is not separate from itself, and as such, the further unveiling of Truth compels the individual seeker into greater union with that which is being sought. The search for the Unknown entails the transformation of the one who asks, revealing answers and realities which could not be perceived by the unmetamorphosized individual alone.

August 27

The Loving Wisdom of Sophia

There is the pain of realizing that we are divided between our deepest desires and the actions that we perform. Each of us knows what it means to suffer something that we do not understand—*Why do we suffer? Is God real, or am I living an illusion?* Yet the hope of transcendence, of higher meaning, of transfiguration, is present even in those moments when we fear we are lost and lack understanding.

We advance through suffering because Spirit wants to strengthen our souls. Sophia, Wisdom, like a mother nurtures us at her breast. She holds us, rocks us, and helps us take our faltering steps. But as we mature, like a good mother, Sophia weans us and sets us on our own path. The soul is purified by the fire of her loving Wisdom. Love itself infuses us with transformation.

August 28

TO MYSTERY ALONE

THE HEART HAS its own Way. The mystical Heart belongs to Mystery alone and does not adhere to any creed, religion, or sect. It transcends reason and stands untouched by mortal mind. The nature of this most holy Reality cannot be comprehended by the intellect nor contained within the limited system of human emotions. This Love touches all and knows the same Truth, being part of the fabric of infinity's mysterious Light.

August 29

The Heart's Divine Claim

All humanity is sustained by the mystical Heart. All people share the inheritance of divine Love, which transcends the specificity of individual belief. Some hearts are wounded, some are fractured and spent; some suffer the illusion of separation and aloneness; others learn to constrict the passageway to infinity—yet all instinctively know its Call and its Message. None escape the Heart's divine claim.

August 30

The Sacred Self

THE MOST MIRACULOUS aspect of the path is that it is impossible not to achieve one's desire. As you ask, so shall you receive: Intense, pure, longing will bring one to Truth. Whether it takes years or lifetimes, each individual is drawn to the sacred self, from whence one has never known separation. Knowing this fact dismantles the despair, the doubt, and the powerlessness we humans carry.

August 31

Woven into the Fabric of the Universe

PERHAPS OF MOST and great importance is our relationship to the Earth, all sentient beings, and the cosmos—who are our monastic mothers, holding our bodies and spirits in the circle womb of creation. We are children of the wind, of water, of air, and of sun and moon. Matter is sanctified and our bodies of flesh are holy vessels. It is tragic that we do not yet comprehend the magnificence of creation, bowing down in awe before the faces of glory in each of us. Yet, if we truly love, we give up and give away the pretense of knowing everything and willing everything—because we recognize that we are woven into the fabric of the universe and everything we do that is in alignment with peace and harmony is of the Holy. We do not truly act. We are the extension in time and space of being acted upon, of the Spirit's breath acting in us.

AUTUMN

September 1

PLEASE HELP ME TO REMEMBER

May all my choices and all my desires
be one with you, Divine Mystery.

As I prepare myself to grow deeper in your love,
please give me the strength
to put aside all my wants and
to receive your intentions for me.

As I move through my day, please help me
to remember your presence in all I do.

Amen

September 2

Living in Sacral Time

An astonishing benefit accrues from giving up the incessant demand for activity and allowing our souls to bask in divine light. By sinking into the holiness of time, the contemplative person makes progress through inaction. Our time can be sacral time. When we follow the rhythm of what is eternal and immaterial, we have entered an enchanted universe—a freedom of being and a sanctuary of rest. Taking a long-term perspective, we recognize the role of patience in following the way of Sabbath, and the blossoming of love in one's heart.

September 3

AN UNCHARTED TERRITORY

IT IS NOT sufficient to know with the mind alone. One must rummage through the pathways of the heart: its hopes, fears, limitations, and sorrows to know oneself, and thus, the eternal. The universe exists within us, and the mechanism for removing human negativity is the heart. The heart speaks no judgment. Neither does it react nor specify limits. The nature of the heart is to be open, receptive, and unconditional. The heart is our divine medium and our window to the absolute. We need not seek the spiritual path with the mind, for the pattern of our divinity shall impose itself upon us. It beckons us, tapping on the closed corridors of our hearts. It is through the heart that we come upon divine passion, and the sparks of creation itself. Through the mind we know the law, but it is through the heart that we embody divinity. The intensity and profound wisdom of the heart is staggering. Because it stands outside of mental constructs, it is the most objective, non-dual, reality we know. And it is a truly uncharted territory of human potential.

September 4

A Global Salvation

A GLOBAL SALVATION has a divine concern with human affairs; it recognizes that something divine is at stake in human existence. All life is holy. No longer content with one's own emancipation, those who seek an inclusive spirituality give themselves over to the reconciliation of our relations and to a bearing of humanity's cruelty and disgrace. We are called to be boldly self-reflective in our errors.

The religions of the world must channel their spiritual resources toward the solution of our planetary problems. They must rediscover the earthly dimension of existence and its spiritual significance in creating a just social, political, and economic order. A peaceful environment is the fruit of justice. It works toward building the right relations and spiritual sensibilities that will guide us toward the inherent birthright of all life: liberation.

September 5

Restoring the Holy Sparks

When the heart becomes a home for the homeless, we participate in the continual rejuvenation of life. Feeling the wound, feeling sorrow, feeling love, but never succumbing to the belief in ultimate estrangement. Never succumbing to rejecting the world as unholy or impure. This world was created in the image of the Divine. We were created in the image of the Divine. Our work is to restore the holy sparks, to continually be a home for the homelessness of the heart.

Divine Love is the answer to all that keeps us separate, small, and divided. It dwells within our deep center, expanding our souls and illuminating our minds with the gift of compassion. Love is freedom itself, the overwhelming gift of cosmic rebirth and renewal.

September 6

The Divine Never Goes Away

We cannot help but live in a paradox where suffering lays down next to joy. We do feel and bear suffering, and not only human or sentient suffering but also divine or mystical suffering. We experience the intentional tearing and destruction of the sacred. We understand in some hidden depth of our hearts that we humans, in a fury of despair, extinguish the hope of the holy coming into our midst. Even as we long for the return of our prophets, bodhisattvas, and messiahs, we refute or deny its possibility in our cells. What are we to do with our hopelessness? Is it a collective grieving and forgetfulness that grips us? Everything we do or do not do reverberates in the whole of creation. Even though we harbor denials and aversions, divinity permeates every thing and is absent from no thing. Our hearts are tuned to the indelible sensitivity intrinsic to each creation; the luminescent light that encloses and encircles life; the scars and wounds we inflict on each other; and the stilling and killing of the sacred that never goes away. We witness the destruction of the holy and it pains our own beings with a grief that we misapprehend and refuse to name. Even though we have been conditioned to be tone deaf to the cries around us and in us that call out for justice and mercy, the Divine never goes away.

September 7

LETTING OURSELVES BE KNOWN

THE MOMENT YOU are known, you become one with the one whom you know. This is the essence of mystical union or intimacy. In high states of contemplation, the Divine opens one's being, and the seeker is known by the all-knowing and the all-knowing knows the seeker.

Every aspect of spiritual growth is related to this important realization. If you pray to open the heart, your life will change. You ask: "What am I protecting? Why don't I want to be known? What do I think is so bad about me that I can't let anyone see?" If you let yourself be known, this is enlightenment. This is sainthood: not hiding, not claiming greatness, simply to be.

September 8

The Divine Spark in the Soul of Creation

We are created to love and to celebrate Divine Mystery in itself and in the bounty of creation. We are created within Divine Heart and everything of the spirit we desire the Divine desires in us. Our being is within Divine Being. Our home is in the House of Holiness. All that we are given and all things we receive are gifts from Divine Mystery. There is nothing that exits that is not spirit. We are given the capacity to know and to love God directly. We discover the Divine in the abundance of the Earth and through the multiplicity of sentient beings. Our journey on Earth is to draw closer to the Divine Mystery so that our hearts become one Heart. Then we are of service in the world. Then we are able to ignite the divine spark in the soul of creation. Compassion and Love—Holy One—may we be Your blessing!

September 9

The Realm of the Beginning

IN CONTEMPLATION, OUR bodies, minds, and spirits dwell in the formless form, the placeless place. This is the realm of the beginning, the womb. Here we are in touch with the archetypes of all spiritual worlds already in existence and those coming into form. We find what Zen practitioners call the "face before we were born." Deep states of contemplation put us in touch with the fundamental traditions, the master structures or master narratives that inform every form of consciousness. These master patterns are encoded in our spiritual bodies like DNA is encoded in our genes. In this depth, contemplation does not refute or eliminate religious and metaphysical distinctions but sees them from the vantage point of their common source or structure, what mystics call "oneness" or "unity." In this mystical depth, the individual is universal or global. What is most important, most prevalent, most real is the unifying force.

September 10

A New Grammar of the Holy

THE CURRENT STATE of our world is requiring of us an emotional honesty that rises from deep currents of feeling—those states deeper than psyche or unconscious that open the soul to wonder and amazement. Something in the touch of the Divine unleashes an emotional torrent that saturates our souls with a new grammar of the holy. We may suppress, deny, or try to kill this depth of feeling, but the compassion intrinsic to our own beings never goes away. We are never free of or far away from a divine level of concern. As the Divine breaks into our hearts, we feel nothing other than the unity that binds all beings together, a flooding of our cells and our senses with the magnitude of being graced. It is like opening every pore in your body, every nerve in your heart, and every fiber of your being to hold and to be embraced by an emotional intensity that can shatter your bones. It is an influx of desire for us and in us that fuels our longing for more; and it comes, when it comes, so often through suffering. The Unconditional advances into our hearts when we are laid bare, when we don't know where else to turn, when we have traded in our membership in the social club for the pain of not belonging and find the courage to just say "Yes." Let me be. Let it all in. Show me what Is.

September 11

Social Witness

THE MOST SUCCESSFUL campaigns to affirm dignity have arisen through the application of nonviolent principles to eliminate concrete instances of injustice and oppression. A contemplative focus alerts us to how violation of spiritual integrity and equality wounds our bodies but also our souls. Nonviolence insists that dialogue must take into account and bring to the world's attention the great sorrow that is generated from collective destruction and abuse of the sacred in our world. Social witness is intrinsic to interfaith spirituality because it is the process by which the oneness with all life can be actualized in our institutions, nations, and relations. Only when we recognize the voices of those who are absent from dialogue because of systematic hunger or social and political oppression will we find the way to truly heal all that prevents God from coming to fullness in the life of the person.

September 12

Gratitude

GRATITUDE OVERFLOWS FROM the simplification of life, the honing of life into what is actually necessary and what really matters. We think, *Well, we can be grateful when we have many things*. But we discover that gratitude is not dependent on externals. It is dependent on our commitment and our desire to love life. Therefore it is within our capacity to achieve gratefulness. It's not dependent on what the world gives us, but rather what we give of ourselves to the world.

Without gratitude, we cannot enter into the heart of reality. Without humility, the soul will be prevented from achieving its great longing. Without giving ourselves away with devotion and love, we cannot enter the tabernacle of the Holy.

September 13

Honoring Solitude

Imagine an inner hermitage in your heart. Center your energies within the heart. Feel the solitude of being with the Holy within. Are your energies centered within your physical body? What would it mean for your energies to not be centered? Where would it be, and can you sense where it is, right now? Cherish your solitude. Embrace your solitude. Imagine being in solitude while in loving relationships. Practice daily.

September 14

Integral Unity

Both interior and exterior to the self, the unity of existence in our own secret center provides a global paradigm for human and planetary sustainability. It does not need to be invented as it is already within us—we are made of and by unity—and no doubt it is already unfolding. It is certainly most completely expressed in the teachings of the seers and saints, whose collective thought forms one of the most sustained meditations on the oneness of existence. For it seems that from whichever corner of the globe, or whatever religious persuasion, the mystic voice speaks out of an integral unity, totally present everywhere without division.

September 15

An Excavation of our Hearts and Minds

We are not here for ourselves alone. It is incumbent upon us to realize how our actions or inactions profoundly affect our soul health, relationship with all beings, and the diverse and complex biosphere of the Earth. We need a voice and a vision from which to awaken the heart of the world and to rescue ourselves from endangering the spirit of life. Injustice and war strike more deeply into the sacred web of creation, generating a hopelessness and despair that wound all our souls. The integrity of our planet and the fate of ecosystems are dependent on an excavation of our hearts and minds—and our souls and spirits—to discover a more generous benevolence and a sturdier vow of humility.

September 16

The Mystical Strength of Love

Love demands total attention and ultimate union with all that is pained, because only in union can sorrow be lifted from human hearts. Here, in this state, resides great mystical strength. As Love unfolds within the heart, one is blessed with a searing compassion that sees the suffering, grief, and injustice of the human condition. But more than seeing, compassion acts, for total observation creates union from which the first pure action arises. Compassion is a dynamic strength; it does not rest dormant within one's heart. It is a vital force that mends all pain, releasing joy into the spiritual atmosphere.

September 17

Our Healing is Sophia's Healing

To reach a depth of spiritual maturity, the person travels the gospel of mercy, the path of profound forgiveness. Images found in mystical writings of the soul's absorption, annihilation, and melting into the Beloved illustrate that the great truth we seek is found in mutual intimacy. This high degree of surrender opens the soul to Sophia's tenderness and benevolence, and the pouring forth of Her mercy into the mighty river that flows between the soul and Divine Love.

Mercy heals our hearts of the violent and punishing way in which we treat each other and creation. It calls us to assert the dignity and worth of every life form and that of our planet. The balm of forgiveness in which the soul is graced is restorative not only to oneself, but to divinity as well. Our healing is Sophia's healing.

September 18

Our Graced Destiny

Intrinsic to being is the presence of the Divine in our depth. This fact is not dependent on acceptance or recognition or faith; instead, it is inherent in us, in a similar way that atoms comprise matter. It means that we can never escape our graced destiny. The Divine within is always present, waiting to be realized. The monk focuses his or her life on this goal: of being one with God, liberated from *samsara*, truly awake. The various practices and virtues that govern a contemplative orientation point the way forward.

September 19

The Dawning Heart Within

The dawning heart within each of us—the heart that is pure spirit—yearns for a moment of selflessness, for a spiritual love without self-interest. Here is where the mystic sight impregnates our bodies and leaves us without a home, for pathos has nowhere to rest its head, except in the arms of every other who is abandoned by the side of the road.

September 20

CONTRADICTION AND PARADOX

CONTRADICTION AND PARADOX are intrinsic to this life. It is possible to receive spiritual illuminations, and even be touched by mystical union, and still be a flawed and struggling personality. We live in contradiction because the human person is not fully formed. We are born to participate in and co-create divinity on Earth. Our flaws, karmas, and sins are part of what we are working to resolve in the world, striving to transform our hearts. We should not be surprised that we still seek to be whole. Our imperfections and sins are not evidence that the Divine is not present with us, that we cannot change things. They are the fuel that motivate prophetic action and teach us about redemption.

Perhaps this is the original human story of tragedy: that we are granted divine life and we are still flawed. But this is what being human entails—we are beings who stand at the juncture of Heaven and Earth, wisdom and ignorance, love and despair. We have to honor both, by having compassion for our foibles and by our willingness to be transformed.

September 21

THE DISCIPLINE OF AGAPE

IN ORDER TO perform the spiritual discipline of *agape* (divine love), we must begin to participate in a way of looking at the world from God's perspective: the passing away of the distinction between self and other, human and Divine, and lover and beloved. Such an orientation requires a continual movement toward the divine emptiness and toward a detachment from the logic of absolutism. The principle of love overturns the law, for it requires of the lawgiver a humility of singular devotion. This is the justice that can be dispensed only through an unmediated, vulnerable encounter with the uniqueness of every other. It is an expression of divine-human intimacy that remains loyal to the openness that underlies every assertion and to the deep vulnerability of our relations.

September 22

Beyond That Which Can Be Spoken

Joyous procession, led by Love, adorns the avenues of Humility, and winds its way into the sacred and mysterious Heart. Anointed and untouched, most beautiful Heart radiates bliss, illuminating all the dimensions with Love.

Beckoned by the Heart and transfixed by the Light, one is absorbed into the eternal soul. Resting within the silence, cushioned by the wondrous joy, one sheds distinction and is no longer alone.

It is here, in the Mystery, that one becomes the eternal Image. It is here where the Unknown anchors itself to form that the self is discarded to begin the journey of Union, beyond the dimensions of the soul, beyond that which can be spoken.

September 23

The Well of Love Within

ANY EFFORT DESIGNED to lift the oppression of one community requires that it also expand beyond tribal and local concerns to include the universe of suffering beings. We are made in the divine image, and our souls are of infinite value. If we accept this moral fact, we must recognize that divine love is real and concrete, that it is the organizing principle of the entire creative universe. Our souls cannot be content to witness hunger and homelessness, to see masses of people victimized by war and ill health. Although the enormity of our global problems can feel overwhelming at the personal level, the challenge is to uncover the well of love within us.

September 24

A Glorious Light

SOMETIMES WE HAVE to make difficult decisions because the world pulls us in contrary directions. But, if we make the choice that deepens spiritual growth, we will build integrity and wisdom. This is because we have been created with the free will to move closer to or away from the Spirit. Listening to the divine call within is vital for understanding the motives beneath our thoughts and actions, and for accepting or rejecting those things the mind proposes for us to do.

Discernment is a lifelong method of measuring the ego's desire against the wisdom of the divine creator, whose glorious light illuminates the mind and acitvates the interior path along which a soul is being led.

September 25

The Greatest Force

SPIRITUAL RIGHTS GIVE specific advocacy to bring into dialogue the effect human rights violations have on the emotional and spiritual health of the person and by extension on the entire global community. Our most profound feelings of what is just and unjust, moral and immoral, truth and falsehood are indicators of the Spirit speaking through us. We are filled with grief, fear, pain, anger, despair, and shame at the great loss and destruction of the holiness of our planet. We cannot and should not suppress this deep emotional anguish, but rather should channel its energy toward reconciliation and alleviation of suffering. It is both a human right and a divine right to be free from spiritual harm.

September 26

The Doorway of Freedom and Truth

It is divine eyes that struggle to see, divine mind that labors to know, and divine heart that longs to love in the midst of human greed, temptation, betrayal, cruelty, and loss of hope. It is this conscious bearing that compels us toward humility, reconciliation, and redemption, from which we are never free and which calls our hearts to relieve each other's suffering and distress. It is this primary imprinting, this stamping of our being with divine being, that leads us to the doorway of freedom and truth.

September 27

Back to the Beginning

Global spirituality brings us back to the beginning, to be co-creators of a new Earth consciousness. Back to the ancient stories within which our ancestors sinned and spoke. Back to the Garden of Eden and the biblical prohibition against knowledge and the punishment of females. Back to the sound of *aum* and the exodus from Egypt. As a new divine-human venture, global spirituality refutes or pays no attention to the various and many attempts of religions to contain and control the Mystery within their own specific and exclusive hierarchical structures. Instead, it goes back to the beginning to rectify the injustices and omissions of our collective religious heritage. It offers itself as a prayer of healing for the historical sins and institutional oppressions of our various religious worldviews. Only then—when we repent for our religious sins and support the dignity of all creation—will we have a "global" spirituality. Riding on the currents of free air, a global spiritual orientation follows this emerging heart to claim a new permission and a new realization of the intrinsic need to love and to be loved.

September 28

Breakthrough

Breakthrough is a sharing in the place where God disrobes and discards property and name. God shares its own unbecoming, and the rapture of indistinction on the other side of nothingness. Nothing is left intact; the radicalness of the movement from light to darkness and from being to unbeing breaks the construction of identity. It is not only the self that is shattered and torn; God is deconstructed and made empty. When the self does not seek refuge in the security of concrete names, the force of divine nothingness liberates being. Mystics who have crossed the borders of nothingness pray—like Meister Eckhart did—for God to free them of God, of all that stands in the way of that vast plane of emptiness where both God and our hearts are undone.

September 29

Women's Spiritual Rights

THE FURTHEST FRONTIER in feminist activism rests with a woman's spiritual rights, and her right to claim herself as representative of the Divine in every area of life. Throughout history women have ceded these rights to male power elites, and to religious professionals who owned and dictated women's relationship with God. In order for women to achieve equality and dignity, legal solutions, religious concessions, or economic advancement is not enough. Women must claim their right to full spiritual equality and work toward its advancement. This demand for justice rises up from a woman's deepest center, where she is one with her divine source. It is, in its most eloquent spiritual form, a claim for human rights.

September 30

Truth

SELF-REALIZATION COMES THROUGH truth, and truth comes through self-restraint. We cannot know truth if we are partial, looking out only for ourselves. Truth sees the whole. It is apprehension of the oneness that underlies diversity. Truth goes to the core, the fundamental reality, the piercing wisdom of ultimate existence. The ability to know truth comes from discipline and self-restraint. It is not something that we can achieve by charisma or self-appointment. It comes from a lifetime of being tested by the fires of desire, by the world's claim on the seeker. It comes from a lifetime of choices and decisions that draw one closer to or further away from truth.

October 1

Unconditional Goodness

SINCE THE SOUL is divine, Gandhi held that humans were good in their core. Self-sacrifice was the method of unlocking goodness in each person. By offering himself as a person of peace and openness—which could entail physical or psychological pain, imprisonment, or even death—he believed the goodness in others would be activated, overriding the power of violence and evil. He held this belief unconditionally, as the philosophical core of his life.

This same principle is at the center of a monastic spirituality: deeper than our errors or sins is unconditional goodness. The belief that we are broken or incomplete is not the ultimate truth. Precisely where we believe ourselves to be unholy or unhealed is the place where the Divine bathes us in love.

October 2

A GOD WITH NO NAME

IT IS NOT an easy road, this wandering away from the road maps and grocery stores of the organized religions. There is always the temptation to tame it and make it palatable to the ardent criticisms that come one's way: this is not a real religion, it is only New Age spirituality, Goddess worship, or a pluralistic smorgasbord of tasty bites from many religions. This path has no authenticity; it traces its lineage back to no certifiable prophet, messiah, or guru. Who could believe it? Who would follow it?

The common ground among these pilgrims is threefold: (1) they uphold the manyness of truth and are uncomfortable with religious languages and liturgical forms that exclude, oppress, or patronize; (2) they are following an authentic spiritual path—often in the dark and without spiritual languages or community support—to what impassions them, to what calls them in the depth of their souls; and (3) in the process, they are giving life to a new lineage of religious truths, to the deep structure of the religious itself, before it is formalized and takes a name—before it is co-opted and saddled with the dogmatism of the religious "ought."

October 3

Modern Sojourners

IN THE HEARTS and minds of modern sojourners, the gestation of new spiritual traditions is taking place, born of the personal yearning and intuitive wisdom of those who have dared to follow the call. This distinctive spiritual journey, which affirms the unity of existence and the universality of faith, is leading us to a new global consciousness and the development of what is alternately termed an interfaith, interspiritual, or interreligious contemplative practice. It is the discovery of a oneness greater than our differences and a common spirituality that heals the divide in human consciousness and, by so doing, provides the sacred foundation for a global culture.

October 4

Radical Normalcy

CONTEMPLATION IS ALWAYS a revolutionary act. It subverts the daily tedium and searches for the kernel of meaning hidden at the center of each thing, It is thus not the talent of a spiritual elite, but the deepest core of silence present in all of us. Its radicalness is also the quest for normalcy and everyday quiet. But for women, especially those who labor to raise children, work, and tend to families, contemplation often becomes a subversive choice. Bombarded daily with conflicting cultural commitments and media images ascribed to females, most women probably do not identify themselves as mytics or believe they are capable of leading a contemplative life. However, unlike our spiritual predecessors, women today do not need to confine themselves to a cloister or cloak themselves in religious clothing to live in a contemplative way.

October 5

Creating a New Language

An incompletely mapped territory, the mystical path of the feminine is more hidden than the language of the Fathers, or the visible religions of male gods and patriarchs. It requires the silent forbearance that prophecy brings—as well as the pain of birthing—before being able to name this gift.

If we are called today to be bearers of the Divine Feminine, then our task is to give words to Her new offering. If religious languages continually diminish, reject, dominate, marginalize, or demonize, if the language of the spirit is spoken almost exclusively in male terms, if God is predominantly He, if prophets are always "he," and if messiahs are singularly embodied in a male person, then language itself betrays what Divine Sophia is.

To bring into speech what we truly know and are, requires both breakthrough and breakdown. We must break into the collective storehouse of memory and retrieve our mother-tongue. Without language, feminine wisdom is lost and its contribution erased with each person's passage from this world. This ancient *lingua feminina* is brought to word through experience and re-inscribed in our minds and hearts each time we name what we truly know.

October 6

Light Beyond Light

IN THE TENSION where we no longer know who and what we are, whether there is a god we dare call God, whether there is anything other than betrayal, comes a Presence, Light beyond Light. This unveiling of our own sacred feminine is nothing less than a reordering of knowing and being. We discover that our true self exceeds religious traditions. From this vantage point, something radical happens: the center of our subjectivity shifts. Touched by the Divine Feminine's liberating voice, we have been named as Her own.

October 7

Participation in the Sacred

What is needed is a new thinking of the religious and a more radical expressing of the mystical that begins from a premise never before considered on a global scale. We need a spirituality profoundly respectful of humanity's diverse participation in the sacred, that is also unifying and humble, rooted in the earth, sustained by the diversity of life forms, and respectful of the emerging wisdom traditions, among them the ecological, liberationist, feminist, developing world, and interspiritual.

October 8

Expressing Our Full Humanity

Our bodies help us to stay grounded on Earth. They teach us to focus and to listen to the wisdom of being physical beings, and to honor the body as a manifestation of Spirit. Through our words, actions and non-actions, and our capacity to love and inspire, we glimpse our potential. Similarly, our psychic intuition attunes us to subtle energy fields that compose sentient life, while our mystical capacity to strive toward oneness points us toward the unseen dimension and to the immense energy of love that forms us. Access to these higher realms of knowing and insight are our birthright; their wisdom is vital not only to every spiritual path, but also to expressing our full humanity.

October 9

Into the Wilderness

Interreligious and interfaith dialogue is the work of the Spirit in us. It is a faith journey that activates the soul's latent desire to grow closer to truth. Individuals who practice interfaith spirituality do not set out to construct a new religion; they are drawn by an interior call to a living faith experience. In the recesses of their own being, they are stirred to enact an openness to others and to step outside the confines of their own stories. As a journey of faith, interreligious spirituality leads us into the wilderness to experience the change of heart, doubt, fear, happiness, and illumination that grip all genuine spiritual seekers.

October 10

EVERY MOMENT IS SACRED

SOLITUDE IS MY tabernacle; silence my prayer. Infinite Mercy has made me without country or home that I may possess nothing, even though she has given me untold riches. She has taught me that the heart cannot be owned nor the spirit tamed, and that God is not a name that can be bought or sold. I travel with her and she with me in regions of intimacy, where my longing is divine longing and love is all there is. Her gentleness is so powerful all sins redeemed, her openness so immense nothing withheld. From her benevolent embrace we are never separate, and in her compassionate heart all truth is known.

October 11

The Mystical Method

The mystical method occurs in the daily events of life. It is not taking place solely in the energy field or the soul. It is activated by the actions and decisions in the life of a person who—like an artist painting a canvas—does not have conscious control of how the brushstrokes lead to a final image. We are generating the actions that will determine whether we embrace the facts and life lessons before us, drawing us closer or further away from a spiritual outcome. We choose how we will advance or retreat. Even when we are not aware of our decisions, we have chosen. Nothing in our existence is separate from this goal.

October 12

God Pours In

What do we offer to the Beloved? Everything: suffering and pain and joy and pleasure. We often think we can only be with God when we are in a good mood, when we have something good to say, when we come with everything polished, our bow tie on or ribbons in our hair. No, it is your afflictions that God wants. When you cry out: God, *where are you? Why have you betrayed me, why have you left me to suffer? I anguish over my imperfections. I don't know you. I don't know how to pray to you. I am angry with you,* these are offerings too, because it is a moment of truth. The Divine can take it.

It is the tumultuous emotions that finally force us to surrender and allow the Beloved into our hearts. When we try to be perfect and polished, we are still in control. But when we offer ourselves in weakness, we pour ourselves out. That is when God pours in.

October 13

Multiple Dimensions of the Sacred

Interfaith dialogue involves a mutual relationship of understanding between partners and a willingness to appreciate the values in other religions and to alter prior misconceptions. To pierce the layer of reason that often distances traditions, partners in dialogue must be willing to enter the sacred depths of other traditions and return with new insight and understanding.

In this interfaith quest, we are reminded of the passion of life to know its source. We realize that we are all called to the banquet of liberation, for no religion has the totality of truth. We need the manyness of religious forms not only to hold a fuller picture of divinity and ourselves, but to humble our hearts. The Divine has chosen to reveal itself in pluralism, in the splendor and beauty of multiple dimensions of the sacred. And yet through the pluralism of religions, we are drawn to the source of silence that transcends and integrates them all. We must insist upon loyalty to the treasures of each other's traditions and at the same time hold in our hearts the mystical desert that is greater than any religion.

October 14

The Seeds of Transformation

We are tasked with making deification—the capacity of each person to achieve holiness—real; that is, living in such a way that the integration and embodiment of the divine-human, especially the relationship of the physical and spiritual, is woven into the fabric of daily life. It means redefining personhood, not as fallen or wandering, but as the self who carries the seeds of transformation and future renewal.

October 15

The Gift of Divine Vulnerability

One of the most compelling aspects of St. Teresa of Avila's wisdom is her insistence on the soul's capacity to empathize with, assume, and transform suffering. Like God bears the world's pain, the fully realized soul participates in the intra-divine suffering when God weeps with our weeping. Through the inner eye of love, the soul is given the gifts of divine vulnerability (to bear the wound of love) and divine strength to resist violence and affliction.

October 16

SATYAGRAHA

THE MYSTICAL PRACTICE of nonviolence is not solely concerned with the negative impact of violence, but with *satyagraha*—the "soul-force" that empowers the life-affirming strength and moral resilience necessary for the conversion of the human heart and the enlightenment of culture.

As the common element in all human cultures and traditions, nonviolence provides a path and an interpretative framework that guides us to analyze and implement methods that prevent the severing of God's presence on Earth. It demands an accounting of how human acts of violence tear at our hearts, lay waste to our souls, and lead us to the brink of despair. It asks how these travesties against the spirit of life contribute to collective grief and afflict us in ways that even now the global community has yet to feel, name, or understand.

October 17

An Intimacy So Profound

Mysticism is a lover's tale in search of the Beloved. It is a tale lived in countless hearts throughout history in all corners of the Earth. It is a simple human story, as old as life itself, of a passion centered in the self's quest for truth. Mystics trace the heart's yearnings for the Other with a love that burns the fabric of being, and that is born from an intensity of life's devotion for itself. Grown in the soil of desire, the mystical quest leads one beyond the normal conventions of existence to that threshold where the ego is shed for an intimacy so profound that all traces of identity are let go.

Mysticism is a term used to describe this canvas upon which the soul points in the wilderness of the heart its passionate return to Source. It is considered to be a transformative experience of one's encounter with divine presence, or more intensely as a union, annihilation, or absorption in the divine nature.

October 18

The inflow of Benevolence

Though we are given to sacrifice ego and identity, we are never outside the circle of reciprocity and the excesses of divine love. These divine gifts do not bind us to surrender for and to a Truth outside us, but are the flowing in of receptivity to a superior grace that can never be repaid. We are not punished or inadequate or tempted or in sin; we are simply given with an abundance that overwhelms and humbles every "self." The inflow of benevolence cancels out debts, wiping away our tears and all the old retributions, karmas, and sins. We can afford moments of happiness because the price—of self—has already been paid. There is no choice now. And once the giving has been truly offered, there are only prayers and tears of gratitude and joy.

October 19

The Vision of Oneness

Oneness is a holy sight. It is a key to the mystery of existence and the source of compassion, generosity, and hope. It is the mystical sight granted that tells us who we are, where we belong, and from whence we come. In a fleeting glimpse, we know and understand how profoundly loved we are, how profoundly connected we are, and how profoundly desired we are. Words only touch the hem of such beauty. The vision of oneness illuminates the mind and heart, it draws us into an experience of glimpsing what the Divine knows and feels, and exposes us to a reality vastly different than the one that scaffolds the ego-self.

October 20

To Be Truly Alive

The first step of humility is to respect at all times the sense of awe felt before the Creator. Drive away your forgetfulness. Be alive to the beauty of the world, and to God's commandments. In veneration of spiritual gifts, our heart is pierced by remorse for all we do not give. But, in relinquishing the ego, and accepting that we will never attain perfection, the soul is drawn into the most intimate mercy. Now, the false self is transcended, freedom floods the soul, and we are truly alive.

October 21

Return to the Beginning

HUMILITY IMPLIES RADICAL trust in divine reality. Even though we yearn for mystical union, we cannot command God to be intimate with us. Humility arises when we realize that the Divine comes freely and in its own time. It is not something that we possess or own. God has plans for you, but they may not be the plans you have; that is humility.

The humble person, who has given up independence and separateness, is contained in the Creator. Drawn into God's inner life, the surrendered soul now perceives that the world and all beings are part of divinity, united in the holy of holies. The mystery of our belonging to the universe of love is that when we are humbled by *ayin*—nothingness—we return to the beginning, in intimacy with God and all creation.

October 22

Sustaining the Contemplative Vision

PART OF BEARING the divinity of the world means to *sustain* the contemplative vision through commitment to prayer, meditation, and other spiritual practices and processes. Equally it must be upheld by a commitment to sustained social transformation that betters the lives of all beings. In learning the difference between transient desires and true needs, we discover a deeper and more lasting generosity and humility.

October 23

Inclusive Spirituality

To be spiritually open entails a risk. It calls for a collective discernment of truth which, paradoxically, occurs within one's own heart. It requires trust. For the words of our past may not be the words by which we access our future. This journey is not a mere extension of religious truths applied to the situations of contemporary life. It is not the adapting or reconfiguring of prior theological systems or knowledge to present circumstances; it does not assume that answers to every current problem can be found in our historical traditions. This new spiritual life necessitates a suspension of religious identity in order to midwife the birth of new traditions in our hearts. Our capacity for sacrificial generosity forms the commitment to a theology for today—to an authentic interreligious, global, and inclusive spirituality.

October 24

To Claim One's Call

While everyone has an intrinsic contemplative core, the person who longs for silence, who desires to be alone with the Divine, and who suffers over injustice already has been chosen to walk the path. The person called to contemplation is, in some ways, an unusual person who is often uncomfortable with the way the world operates. Rather than a detriment, it can be healthy to not belong and to be alone, because in solitude we find the heart of hearts, the inextinguishable flame that burns brightly and forever.

To claim one's call to a passion greater than earthly ones is to finally come to terms with your mission in life. This is the mission to seek the Divine that underlies every other activity or choice, a commitment that will reform your being into a new creation. It is not for the easily discouraged, nor for the person who gives up without a struggle, or the one who waits to be told it is okay—go ahead. It is instead for the one who cannot live in the old way; for the person who aspires to and cries out for freedom; for the one who longs to live in and for the Holy.

October 25

A Revelation of Love

THE DIVINE CAN do nothing other than grieve over human violence and simultaneously show us how to transform violence into nonviolence. The silence that is at the core of our being labors to draw us into the heart of mercy and compassion. In contemplation, we experience the harmony of being, and a peace that transcends understanding. We feel silence permeating personhood and have reverence for the dignity of every being. Peace is a grace and a gift. We cannot conquer or demand it. We discover and unveil peace in our depth: a revelation of love, goodness, hope, beauty, and faith.

October 26

Self-Transcendence

An interior process of transformation and self-transcendence is imprinted in the soul of every person. Our existence as living beings is in motion toward holiness and divinization, a fact that innumerable life events seek to subvert. And, yet, the process of self-transcendence echoes a constant vibration deep within the cells of the body and the energies of consciousness. It is never absent; it is never withdrawn. It is enclosed within silence and expressed in awe.

October 27

Life is a Sacrament

SACRAMENT IS PART of existence; only we humans can dim its light or deny its power. Holiness is made new now, every day, and it dwells in each one of us who—branded by the torrent of light—lay our hearts down in stilled expectation and hope.

The Spirit dwells among us and we cannot stop its flow. The saffron-robed Buddhists who climbed over the crooked roads and steep hills of Cambodia to anoint the trees and to ordain the monks knew this. So did Ansel Adams, as he scaled the steep cliffs of Yosemite in tennis shoes to capture a vision of Cathedral Rock. Or Georgia O'Keeffe, who transfixed the hills of Abiquiu on canvases crossed by spirit-translucent light. And the pounding waves on the shore of Mount Tamalpais, which bring us to our knees and salt away our tears. Sacrament is not confined to synagogue or mosque, but flows out into the world for those with eyes to see and hearts to feel.

October 28

Live Love on its Own Terms

IT IS IN the heart and the mind that we carry the sacred call of contemplation. While we may think the Holy is beyond us, so difficult to attain, it is simply a veil away. The more we desire nothingness, the more we are loving and kind, the veil between earthly and heavenly worlds dissolves and we discover the poetic wonder of Creation. When we carry God in our hearts, we may endure but not succumb to the pain of our world. Contemplation is the aspiration to live love on its own terms, carrying within us the fragrance of the beautiful and the holy.

October 29

Simplicity of Life

Practicing simplicity in one's life involves distinguishing between want and need. It asks that we examine our conscience and the ways we buy and sell, hoard and consume. It is an examined life because we choose to examine it. We examine our choices from a place of joy and because we would like our life to be a testimony to peace and a witness to structural and cultural inequities.

Simplicity is an awareness and attention to all of our resources, including the natural world, material possessions, clothing, food, drink, and other kinds of physical objects. It is about how we steward these resources and conserve them for the benefit of all beings. Simplicity of life is not about denial, but implies discernment, attention, and awareness about what we actually need. We practice voluntary simplicity to honor and value the labor of others, to stay focused on our true intentions, and to be more modest in living our daily lives.

October 30

A Way of Being

CONTEMPLATION IS THE most natural way of living in our interiority. It is coming home. It is where we feel most comfortable. An organic process that orients the inner life, and a way of being, contemplation is the essence of our nature. When we bear divinity, we participate in and contribute to the organic and natural growth of reality. Our personal lives and the Divine life exist inside each other and in our co-bearing, we cooperate in the building of a spiritual society on Earth.

October 31

Birth

One meaning of the word "bearing" is to give birth. In the contemplative life, we give birth to deeper dimensions of our souls, and deeper dimensions of the divine nature. We give birth to new insight. We *are* a birthing. We bring forth in our own lives and hearts the sacred presence. Each time we make a choice for openness, love, mercy, compassion, and nonviolence, we are divinizing the world. Birth is tangible, involving cells, bodies, emotions, and thought. It is also mysterious. Here, our theological focus shifts from transcendence, hierarchy, and omnipotence to embodiment, mutuality, and intimacy. Contemplation is birthed in us, body, mind, and soul, and we bear its wisdom in our daily lives.

November 1

A Torrent of Desire

THE MYSTICAL COMES unexpectedly—who could plan or design it?—outside and beyond what we accept or reject. It cannot be held or possessed. Rarely can it even be invoked. Awe comes, we know not how, in the woods beside still oaks, by the bed of a dying parent or friend, in the winter of our anguish when we have lost all hope, on the slope where the setting sun dips beneath the rising crest of an ocean wave. It claims us for its own, touching the depth of our beings, animating the cells of our bodies, and enflaming our longing for the inviolable.

We are impassioned by the wonder of existence itself. We cannot even hold the immensity in our bodies for more than moments, and if we could we would not be born. The mystical flows through our veins and spills into our hearts in a torrent of desire, longing through us for the coming realization or enlightenment. It upends everything, throwing our rationed offerings and our critical analyses against the heart overwhelmed by splendor. We want to know what love would do . . . *What would love do?* That is the mystical.

November 2

Compassion in Action

Compassion is an inner strength and a divine capacity in us that provides the courage to resist suffering and injustice, and to fight despair. The ability to oppose the debilitating effects of hardship and pain is a power of the soul derived from the dignity of all beings, granted by our Creator. Compassion recognizes that humans are *imago dei*, made in the image of God. Because compassion acts to overcome suffering, the quest for reconciliation is an inherent activity of compassion. *I feel that you are suffering, and I will struggle with you to overcome the source of your pain.* This is compassion in action, healing our wounds. When we pray not only for ourselves, but also for those who have harmed us, and sincerely want their freedom from pain, then we are blessed by Mercy. Creation is beautiful and yet tragic at times. True justice is merciful, remaining aware that the ravages of sin always are healed together with our brokenness. Suffering exists because of this brokenness. As we strive to transform pain, compassion imbues us with its spiritual power.

November 3

Why We Pray to be Empty

Humility inspires devotion, and devotion spreads the fragrance of humility. As we become small before awe, our spirit—directly due to the divine will—grows mighty, healing pain and restoring hope. In a sense, the devoted displace themselves in order for the Divine to flow in. It is this longing to prostrate before the divine immensity that ignites mercy and unconditional love.

The antidote to the ego and impaired self-importance is the virtue of humility. Why do we make ourselves less? Why do we pray to be empty? It is out of love. It is out of love that we give away the false self. When light shines on our errors, and we see ourselves through divine eyes, we yearn to be that person through whom the holy is reflected and expressed. We will give all of our mistakes away in order to experience the infinite, all-abiding love that made us.

November 4

Humbly Follow the Path

Intellectual knowledge is of little benefit if the soul does not know truth and cannot direct its energies toward perfecting the soul's virtues. The reason that healing takes place, the reason that consciousness is transformed, is because the experience of selflessness is transmitted from one person to another. Thus, the method of growth for a teacher or knower of spiritual things is to deepen the contemplative life. As the self is deepened, the person is a teaching. To humbly follow the path is itself both the way and the end. This is true wisdom.

November 5

All Life is Holy

Every sentient being is dependent on every other reality for its existence. To speak of life on Earth without holding the mutuality of existence as an essential fact is to be deluded. And, further, we must consider this: How much mourning, grieving, and suffering have we sustained by the absence of the sacred in the public sphere or the refusal to sustain love in relationship?

We are not educated or trained to be highly sensitive to the energetic integrity and mystical responsibility we bear. We are seldom in touch with the awe radiating from each face, the holy mantle encasing every living form. We are often clueless and brutal in our interactions with each other. We do not realize the extent of the damage we inflict, and the tearing of our hearts, caused by our refusal to accept that all life is truly and literally, holy.

November 6

TRUE INTIMACY

THERE IS AN element of illusion in love relationships. It is the belief reinforced by society and commercialism—as well as by religious norms—that union with another person is, or should fulfill every soul desire and be, the sum total of the person's connection in this life. While we intuitively know this is not possible, many people live out their lives as if it were. But here is where monastic wisdom helps re-orient our belief. True intimacy arises when each person maintains his or her center in solitude with the Divine, at the same time that he or she is receptive to uniting with another person in love.

November 7

A Testimony of the Heart

THE ANTIDOTE OF feeling unloved is to love. The antidote for feeling that you do not have enough is to give. The antidote for being attached to self—selfishness—is to practice generosity. These practices will allow you to scale the illusory wall of deprivation that has developed in your soul. The love you have not received in your life can be given to others as a test and testimony of the heart.

November 8

Restful Awareness

IN THE SPIRITUAL traditions we talk about active and passive contemplation. Active contemplation refers to everything we do to bring ourselves closer to God—meditative practices, study, prayer. Passive contemplation is not the absence of positive motion. Rather, it is the action of the Divine in your being. It is God's work in you. It is here that we surrender to the Divine within, sinking into the state of restful awareness. We listen to the Voice: *Come this way. Rest in me.* Agitation ceases, emotions steady.

November 9

Her Sacred Rivers

The path of the Divine Mother embraces the wisdom of every religion and spiritual practice, clarified and empowered by the richness of humanity's collective spiritual heritage. Her revelation leads adherents to the highest states of contemplative consciousness, and to the secret teachings of love. In surrendering your heart to her immediacy, your depth—which is also her depth—subsumes all spiritual truths. All religions flow in the current of Her sacred rivers.

November 10

A Threshold for Another Way

What if the Holy One—Blessed Be She—called us to a new contemplative path and a new way of life? What if She were drawing us closer to a deep cavern of truth that we could only find were we to temporarily give up all of our ideas and notions of God, and place all of our historical understanding of the spiritual life under the *cloud of forgetting*? What if the very spiritual paths we have followed and practiced through the centuries were but a threshold for another way of being and loving? Would we not find the courage to cross over to the splendor to which our Beloved Mother is calling?

November 11

Our Life is Our Teacher

THERE IS NO part of us—neither wound of soul, personal failing, or sins—that is not of great value in helping uncover our true selves. We learn to approach the veils and shields of the false self with detachment and love. We discover that all violation of truth is an aberration of the Great Mystery within us. We thus become excavators of our own truth, digging through the rubble of our anguish, confusion, and missed opportunities for the keys to where and how the spirit has been repressed or denied. Our life—in all of its wonder and pain—is our teacher. It is through the process of spiritual awareness, love, and humility that we discover holiness within.

November 12

TRUE FREEDOM

LIFE IS MOVEMENT; life is infinite openness, relinquishing the limits of self-identity in each moment. But realize that opening to all life means opening to every feeling: despair, fear, anger, survival, betrayal, abandonment, jealousy; as well as joy, love, grace, desire, peace. Be open to feelings. Let them pour out, be willing to bear suffering. This is true freedom because this is life.

November 13

Emptying

All authentic spirituality seeks to ennoble the self. The notion of emptying of the ego empties our concept of humanness. We sacrifice self-identity for the Divine, for the greater good. We offer unto the Ultimate our limited self, in gratitude for the gift of the immeasurable. This, then, is our true mystical path. This is our way of life. It is beautiful. Even physical death is another expression of divinity because it is the ultimate self-emptying possible as a bodily form on Earth. We not only die every moment to self-identity, we not only die every day to personality, but we ultimately relinquish precious human life itself. Even this is a gift of participating in the universal process. Both living and dying are essential.

November 14

THE PATH OF THE HEART

THE CALL IS beckoning, and it is very quiet. It is so still that it only can be heard in solitude and silence. Then: You are simultaneously calling and being called. You are both separate and one, blessed by Love's desire and following the wayless way. When we ask, "Why has God forsaken us?" the truth is that we have forsaken God. God has never forsaken us. The Path of the Heart yearns for totality, to be in union again.

How wonderful to be called!

November 15

All Life is One

Nonviolence is a state of consciousness that sees reality from the perspective of the whole. It recognizes that oneness underlies diversity and searches for ways to protect the unity of life in the concrete situations of every day. When the web of union is disturbed, our hearts overflow with concern and grief. At the same time, there is a spiritual power of the soul that transforms despair into hope and oppression into liberation. It is because the Divine is infinite oneness that we are touched by compassion and are compelled to rectify through nonviolent acts of resistance the cruelty, insensitivity, and injustice inflicted on our brothers and sisters, and to translate this into a desire to alleviate our suffering world.

This ability to empathize with another sentient life rests on a mystical capacity to identify with the suffering of others and to find in that suffering the call for a higher truth. So powerful is this truth—that all life is one—that we must always seek it through struggle and persistent effort. To know the world as the Divine knows us is to risk losing the illusion of a separated and independent self.

November 16

The Mission of Our Life

Spiritual nonviolence begins deep within the soul and is an active expression to love in a new way, to be more holy. This profound vision of life is dependent on the human capacity to love more, give more, and care more for the world. Illuminated in this way, the heart is enflamed by a divine longing to make our planet a place where love can flourish. The vow to be a person of nonviolence means that the mission of our life is directed toward actualizing the promise of all the world's religions—that we can achieve spiritual harmony on Earth.

November 17

VAST INTIMACY

TO HAVE ANY identifiable name, even one as collaborative as "Interfaith," can be problematic. As soon as an idea or vision takes form, there are people who want to domesticate and possess it or make it something sustaining, permanent, enduring, respectable, transmittable, something capable of being organized and, therefore, controlled. But how do you contain a *vantage point*—seeing everything from the perspective of vast intimacy such that all things are included within it, all determinate religions are the children of this immense dynamism?

November 18

Seeing

When the mystic heart looks at creation, it sees the world is formed by and composed of a divine imprint everywhere present and nowhere absent. Nothing that *is*, is not spirit. This is what the mystic in us *sees*; this is what the mystic in us *knows*; it is this that compels the mystic in us to celebration and lament. Sadly, we have been educated and trained to close our hearts and avert our eyes from the blazing light all around us.

We pass our blindness and muteness down from generation to generation, as if we tell our newborns: *Don't see. See at your own peril.* We learn early on to hide our wisdom, to be ashamed of our vision, to suffer ridicule for our sensitivity or insight: *Don't know. Don't tell too much*. It is not the mystical that is a secret, hidden realm. It is the hiding and blinding and denying that is killing us. This is the secret that we do not want to see or hear: we are socially conditioned to be "unsee-ers."

November 19

DIVINE-HUMAN HARMONY

WHAT IS THE method, the process of liberation that is the foundation of contemplative formation? It involves striving toward purity of heart, to become part of the cosmic interpenetration of realities and gradually embody in this life the goal of divine-human harmony. It is the juxtaposition of suffering and exaltation, of renunciation and abundance, of humility and glory, of weakness and strength, etc.—all of these seeming dichotomies taking place within the infinite depths of being in every one of us. It is the contemplative process that moves the person—sometimes slowly and inexorably, sometimes radically all at once—to the farther shore, to finally experience reality as it is.

November 20

What Matters

Every spiritual path advances according to the two most important aspects of the inner journey: love of truth alone and emptiness of self. When we put our whole self and our whole passion on love of the Divine, we belong then to the sphere of the holy. It does not matter if we know where we are going or are lost or even have a god with a name. What matters is that we finally give ourselves over to the Spirit. By concentrating our whole self on love and longing for Truth, we forge a path toward the open days of awe. In this way we learn from the interior of our souls; we are taught through the hidden ground of love about spiritual things and the true nature of reality. To love in this way requires the absence of self-interest; it requires a giving away of the false self in order to melt into emptiness or nothingness.

November 21

Mystical Knowledge

COMPASSION ARISES FROM a mystical or contemplative knowledge that wishes to know others as we are known by our Creator. Although another person's experience is not fully accessible to us, we are able to mystically share in their heartbreak and celebrate their good fortune and success. By our concern for others, we participate in and mirror the Holy Mother's loving, tender care. Compassion is suffering with another because our heart has become vulnerable and able to bear pain. This is not sympathy, in the sense of merging with another. True compassion is more detached, it knows through the wisdom of the heart—having been made simple and empty—and is capable of being with the wounded and effecting healing change.

November 22

The Monastic Ideal

As a global community it is helpful to reimagine our world as a spiritual monastery, in which the sacredness of the Earth and our life within it are considered in their holiness. Like the traditional monk, we are called to uphold an impossible ideal—the coming into our lives of paradise, of the hoped for communion and unity of hearts. This ability to see each other as brother and sister, and to practice compassion, peace, mercy, and forgiveness, provides nourishment for body and soul. We need to cultivate the monastic ideal of living for Spirit, rather than for human ends, transposing this monastic worldlessness from the individual or group to the well-being of the whole earthly community.

November 23

HELD WITHIN A MATRIX OF MEANING

SOUL WOUNDS PROVIDE a glimpse into the generous gift of grace—that every wound exists against the backdrop of infinite love. We experience fractures because they are reflected in the mirror of what is whole and untarnished. We feel the pain of failings because they are embraced and upheld by mercy. Whatever the person does to move away from their divine source, the way to healing and restoration is through the original disavowal, through recognizing the injustice that has been suffered and moving back to the center, not avoiding it.

Wounding, even the pain of sin, is held within a matrix of meaning that is wholly and utterly on the side of love. Love is at the center of being; our essential core is pure, verdant, growing love. The Divine reaches down into every suffering and lifts us up.

November 24

Perfect Love

In the beginning, we are infused with perfect love. Whenever we experience unqualified love for another, we swim in the ocean of divinity; we draw from the root of being. We are bathed in warmth; endearingly embraced. Imprinted in us is a higher understanding of spiritual love, a love without self-interest that is concerned for the good of others. By the steadfast desire breathed into us from our origins in the Divine, we are instilled with a capacity to know and feel unconditional love, and to suffer in its absence.

Love is a real force or energy. It can be transmitted; it is cumulative. Because we are composed of perfect love, we can harness its energies to motivate action and change. We should always remember that its source is already present within us.

November 25

Gift of Grace

Compassion is the ability to perceive intuitively the secrets of another's heart. This power is not psychic intuition, but the fruit of grace and mystical insight that helps to unveil the hidden depths, which the seeker does not speak of or may be unaware. This is taking into one's soul the soul of another, praying for their wholeness and healing. The compassionate person truly desires the happiness of all beings and works to free others from suffering by transforming conditions that harm life, wherever they exist. When we meditate on the nature of suffering, we grow in spiritual wisdom, recognizing that all pain is transitory and impermanent in the heart of the Holy One. The practice of compassion and mercy is so profound that we cannot measure its benefit.

November 26

Spiritual Nonviolence

Nonviolence is a way of life and a mystical practice based on centuries-old traditions of inner peace. It is motivated by a keen sense of both the fragileness and resilience of human communities and taps into the river of wisdom that guides us to recognize the spiritual rights and dignity of every person and sentient being.

Spiritual nonviolence derives power and efficacy from its theological foundation in divine love. It is never for social transformation without soul transformation. It is especially concerned with the spiritual implications of nonviolence on the inner life and growth of the seeker. For this reason, the word "nonviolence" is modified with "spiritual" to underscore the self-awareness and personal repentance that is critical to changing our hearts.

November 27

The Holy Circle of Compassion

COMPASSION CHALLENGES US to new ways of living, new ways of speaking, new ways of knowing, new ways of sharing, and new ways of being intimate. It repudiates force, coercion, and domination. To some, compassion appears weak, meek, or lowly, but this is actually mystery: its apparent weakness is its strength. Its humility is its power. Its silence is its command. Its bearing of suffering is its healing ability. Compassion engenders humility and loss of ego. In that one moment of experiencing your goodness—not because you have done something good or because someone else says that you are good, but because you were created and were given life—you belong to the holy circle of compassion.

November 28

Called to Vulnerability

Contemplation on nonviolence is founded on a theology of love. It reveals the inner life of the Divine, which is infinite openness, infinite mercy, infinite peace, infinite oneness, and infinite love.

Infinite Openness calls us to be vulnerable to life and to each other. If we wish to understand and practice nonviolence, we must be willing to participate fully in life, to listen to each other, to communicate, dialogue, and receive. The divine attributes of vulnerability and intimacy are inherent in our depth, activated whenever we open our hearts and minds to the wonder of the world.

November 29

Transforming the Spiritual Journey

Contemplation is always revolutionary, for it takes apart what is comfortable and convenient, asking us to see the world from God's perspective. Applied to feminist concerns, it protests the fragmentation and distraction of women's lives and repudiates the selfless renunciation that is women's daily lot in much of the world. Further, it challenges the rampant materialism that makes women's bodies and the body of creation objects to be bought and sold.

The fact that the spiritual journey itself is dominated by patriarchal thinking, unjust relations, or oppression of women and feminine states of consciousness indicates that there is a dimension of the soul that is not free, a place where we have not yet found total redemption, salvation, liberation, or enlightenment. The injustices that taint the religious imagination of Western culture are found in the spiritual as well—its techniques of enlightenment, roles assigned to women, areas of practice taught, kinds of spiritual experiences given credibility, and images of the Divine sought.

November 30

The Path of Enlightenment

LOOKING BACK OVER the span of our lives, there always has been a part of us that was ready to take up a begging bowl and follow wherever we were led. Because the whole point of enlightenment rests on this: Trust the inner voice, love the Divine with one's whole heart, and be empty of self.

Title References

Each day's entry is taken from Beverly Lanzetta's published books, unpublished journals and lectures, or meditations posted on the author's website, beverlylanzetta.net. Occasionally, entries are edited or otherwise adapted from the original published work. Thus, researchers are encouraged to cite the version and page numbers appearing in *Sacred Seasons*.

Beverly Lanzetta's published books listed in this reference, with abbreviations:

OSN *The Other Side of Nothingness: Toward a Theology of Radical Openness.* Albany: State University of New York Press, 2001.

RW *Radical Wisdom: A Feminist Mystical Theology.* Minneapolis: Fortress Press, 2005.

EH *Emerging Heart: Global Spirituality and the Sacred.* Minneapolis: Fortress Press, 2007.

NJN *Nine Jewels of Night: One Soul's Journey into God.* San Diego: Blue Sapphire Books, 2014.

POH *Path of the Heart: A Spiritual Guide to Divine Union.* San Diego: Blue Sapphire Books, 2015.

TMW *The Monk Within: Embracing a Sacred Way of Life.* Sebastopol: Blue Sapphire Books, 2018.

ANS *A New Silence: Spiritual Practices and Formation for the Monk Within.* Sebastopol: Blue Sapphire Books, 2020.

FOP *A Feast of Prayers: Liturgy to Holy Mystery.* Sebastopol: Blue Sapphire Books, 2021.

W Website

UL Unpublished Lecture

DECEMBER

1 Dec RW, 212-213
2 Dec POH, 109
3 Dec ANS, 15-16
4 Dec RW, 203
5 Dec TMW, 254
6 Dec TMW, 289-290
7 Dec NJN, 68-69
8 Dec TMW, 203-204
9 Dec ANS, 189
10 Dec LANS, 228
11 Dec ANS, 324
12 Dec TMW, 154
13 Dec EH, 128-129
14 Dec RW, 196
15 Dec OSN, 129
16 Dec TMW, 135-136
17 Dec TMW, 154-155
18 Dec TMW, 155
19 Dec UL, 2014
20 Dec W, 6/20/2018
21 Dec TMW, 17
22 Dec TMW, 133-134
23 Dec RW, 195
24 Dec OSN, 107
25 Dec ANS, 321-322
26 Dec TMW, 17
27 Dec TMW, 156-157
28 Dec TMW, 156-157
29 Dec W, 2/24/2016
30 Dec W, 2/24/2016
31 Dec W, 3/2/2016

JANUARY

1 Jan POH, 20-21
2 Jan NJN, 227
3 Jan TMW, 282-283
4 Jan TMW, 96
5 Jan EH, 121-122
6 Jan POH, 92-93
7 Jan TMW, 220-221
8 Jan POH, 33-34
9 Jan POH, 128
10 Jan TMW, 350
11 Jan EH, 41-42
12 Jan TMW, 139-140
13 Jan POH, 100
14 Jan TMW, 70-71
15 Jan TMW, 69
16 Jan OSN,129
17 Jan W, 12/20/2018
18 Jan ANS, 174
19 Jan W, 12/6/2018
20 Jan TMW, 310
21 Jan TMW, 251-253
22 Jan TMW, 59
23 Jan TMW, 60
24 Jan POH, 105-106
25 Jan EH, 129-130
26 Jan TMW, 68
27 Jan OSN, 99
28 Jan TMW, 64-65
29 Jan OSN, 120, 131
30 Jan TMW, 15
31 Jan UL, 2015

FEBRUARY

1 Feb TMW, 348, 355 & FOP, 1
2 Feb EH, 117
3 Feb TMW, 264
4 Feb TMW, 216-217
5 Feb TMW, 199
6 Feb TMW, 198
7 Feb TMW, 208
8 Feb TMW, 91
9 Feb POH, 158
10 Feb OSN, 121
11 Feb ANS, 37-38
12 Feb W, 7/12/2017
13 Feb EH, 85-86
14 Feb TMW, 13
15 Feb TMW, 129
16 Feb TMW, 130
17 Feb POH, 99
18 Feb EH, 65-67
19 Feb TMW, 89-90
20 Feb TMW, 89-90
21 Feb TMW, 255-256
22 Feb UL, 2000
23 Feb TMW, 155
24 Feb ANS, 166
25 Feb W, 12/14/2016
26 Feb W, 12/14/2016
27 Feb TMW, 68
28,
29 Feb RW, 212

MARCH

1 Mar FOP, 32-33
2 Mar ANS, 167
3 Mar EH, 114-115
4 Mar EH, 130
5 Mar TMW, 333
6 Mar EH, 88
7 Mar EH, 124
8 Mar NJN, 11
9 Mar UL, 2012
10 Mar TMW, 190-191
11 Mar NJN, 129
12 Mar EH, 35
13 Mar TMW, 16
14 Mar POH, 111
15 Mar POH, 112
16 Mar TMW, 258
17 Mar ANS, 323-324
18 Mar W, 2/5/2016
19 Mar W, 2/5/2016
20 Mar ANS, 315-316
21 Mar ANS, 35
22 Mar W, 1/21/2016
23 Mar W, 11/19/2015
24 Mar ANS, 150
25 Mar ANS, 151
26 Mar ANS, 151
27 Mar ANS, 151
28 Mar ANS, 153
29 Mar ANS, 148
30 Mar ANS, 153
31 Mar UL, 2019

APRIL

1 Apr	FOP, 38-39
2 Apr	ANS, 154-155
3 Apr	ANS, 157
4 Apr	ANS, 157-158
5 Apr	ANS, 158
6 Apr	W, 6/24/2015
7 Apr	FOP, 58
8 Apr	W, 5/20/2015
9 Apr	W, 5/20/2015
10 Apr	TMW, 146-148
11 Apr	TMW, 146-148
12 Apr	W, 5/14/2015
13 Apr	UL, 2019
14 Apr	W, 4/29/2015
15 Apr	W, 4/24/2015
16 Apr	W, 4/24/2016
17 Apr	FOP, i-ii
18 Apr	POH, 129
19 Apr	POH, 129-130
20 Apr	ANS, 197
21 Apr	RW, 95
22 Apr	POH, 169-170
23 Apr	POH, 170-171
24 Apr	POH, 103-104
25 Apr	POH, 63-64
26 Apr	POH, 165-166
27 Apr	POH, 165-166
28 Apr	POH, 161-162
29 Apr	TMW, 72
30 Apr	EH, 196

MAY

1 May	RW 204
2 May	OSN, 123
3 May	ANS, 53-154
4 May	ANS, 154
5 May	ANS, 69
6 May	ANS, 155
7 May	ANS, 155
8 May	ANS, 286-287
9 May	ANS, 286-287
10 May	ANS, 286-287
11 May	TMW, 57, 150
12 May	ANS, 50
13 May	ANS, 190-191
14 May	OSN, 3-4
15 May	ANS, 304-305
16 May	TMW, 349
17 May	RW, 32-33
18 May	RW, 42
19 May	ANS, 218
20 May	POH, 127
21 May	OSN, 127
22 May	TMW, 164
23 May	ANS, 214
24 May	RW, 165
25 May	EH, 47
26 May	TMW, 352
27 May	TMW, 103
28 May	RW, 31
29 May	EH, 32
30 May	NJN, 103
31 May	NJN, 102

JUNE

1 Jun	ANS, 32
2 Jun	POH, 106-107
3 Jun	POH, 125
4 Jun	W, 2014
5 Jun	W, 2014
6 Jun	FOP, 60
7 Jun	W, 2014
8 Jun	W, 2014
9 Jun	W, 2014
10 Jun	W, 2014
11 Jun	W, 2014
12 Jun	W, 2014
13 Jun	W, 2014
14 Jun	W, 2014
15 Jun	W, 2014
16 Jun	W, 2014
17 Jun	W, 2014
18 Jun	TMW, 38 & EH, 101
19 Jun	W, 2014
20 Jun	W, 2014
21 Jun	W, 2/19/2000
22 Jun	W, 2014
23 Jun	W, 2014
24 Jun	EH, 116
25 Jun	EH, 55
26 Jun	W, 2014
27 Jun	W, 2014
28 Jun	W, 2014
29 Jun	TMW, 18-19
30 Jun	UL, 2014

JULY

1 Jul	W, 2014
2 Jul	W, 2014
3 Jul	TMW, 200 ff.
4 Jul	W, 2014
5 Jul	TMW, 17
6 Jul	Unpublished
7 Jul	ANS, 103
8 Jul	W, 2008
9 Jul	W, 2008
10 Jul	TMW, 303 ff.
11 Jul	EH, 30
12 Jul	EH, 33
13 Jul	POH, 3
14 Jul	TPOH, 4-5
15 Jul	EH, 110-113
16 Jul	EH, 113-114
17 Jul	NJN, 200-201
18 Jul	ANS, 286
19 Jul	UL
20 Jul	UL
21 Jul	UL
22 Jul	UL
23 Jul	UL
24 Jul	UL
25 Jul	TMW, 146-147
26 Jul	TMW, 147
27 Jul	TMW, 147
28 Jul	TMW, 148-149
29 Jul	TMW, 146
30 Jul	UL
31 Jul	TMW, 236

AUGUST

1 Aug UL
2 Aug ANS, 313
3 Aug UL, 2013
4 Aug ANS, 314
5 Aug TMW, 101
6 Aug UL, 2013
7 Aug ONS, 130
8 Aug RW, 190, 192
9 Aug POH, 72-73
10 Aug UL, 2013
11 Aug POH, 56-57
12 Aug POH, 55-56
13 Aug OSN, 82
14 Aug UL, 2013
15 Aug POH, 34-35
16 Aug EH, 59, 61
17 Aug RW, 31-32
18 Aug RW, 7-11
19 Aug ANS, 312-313
20 Aug POH, 77-78
21 Aug POH, 112-113
22 Aug ONS, 44-45
23 Aug EH, 39
24 Aug EH, 41
25 Aug EH, 21
26 Aug POH, 16-17
27 Aug ANS, 219
28 Aug POH, 13
29 Aug POH, 12
30 Aug POH, 7
31 Aug ANS, 124-125

SEPTEMBER

1 Sep ANS, 92
2 Sep TMW, 213
3 Sep POH, 9
4 Sep OSN, 130
5 Sep TMW, 160
6 Sep EH, 40
7 Sep ANS, 278
8 Sep W, 5/13/2020
9 Sep EH, 119
10 Sep EH, 38-39
11 Sep EH, 106
12 Sep TMW, 292
13 Sep ANS, 307
14 Sep EH, 60-61
15 Sep TMW, 129
16 Sep POH, 29-30
17 Sep TMW, 89
18 Sep ANS, 5
19 Sep EH, 47
20 Sep TMW, 211
21 Sep OSN, 90
22 Sep POH, 80
23 Sep ANS, 46
24 Sep ANS, 140
25 Sep RW, 209
26 Sep RW, 173
27 Sep EH, 130-131
28 Sep OSN, 22
29 Sep RW, 175-176
30 Sep TMW, 155

OCTOBER

1 Oct TMW, 259
2 Oct EH, 56
3 Oct EH, 57
4 Oct RW, 168
5 Oct TMW, 94-95
6 Oct TMW, 93
7 Oct EH, 59
8 Oct TMW, 120
9 Oct EH, 87
10 Oct NJN, 110
11 Oct ANS, 93-94
12 Oct TMW, 176
13 Oct OSN, 110
14 Oct ANS, 5
15 Oct ANS, 215
16 Oct ANS, 43
17 Oct OSN, 15-16
18 Oct EH, 42-43
19 Oct OSN, 98
20 Oct ANS, 17
21 Oct ANS, 17-18
22 Oct RW, 205
23 Oct OSN, 122
24 Oct ANS, 87-88
25 Oct ANS, 42
26 Oct ANS, 93
27 Oct EH, 25-26
28 Oct ANS, 65
29 Oct ANS, 59
30 Oct ANS, 64
31 Oct ANS, 63-64

NOVEMBER

1 Nov EH, 37-38
2 Nov ANS, 36
3 Nov ANS, 26
4 Nov ANS, 30-31
5 Nov ANS, 109-110
6 Nov ANS, 113
7 Nov TMW, 169
8 Nov TMW, 199
9 Nov ANS, 75
10 Nov ANS, 77
11 Nov TMW, 120
12 Nov POH, 128
13 Nov POH, 146
14 Nov POH, 155
15 Nov ANS, 50
16 Nov ANS, 47
17 Nov EH, 21
18 Nov EH, 36
19 Nov ANS, 93
20 Nov EH, 120-121
21 Nov ANS, 37
22 Nov EH, 123
23 Nov ANS, 208
24 Nov TMW, 140-141
25 Nov ANS, 40
26 Nov ANS, 43
27 Nov ANS, 39
28 Nov ANS, 48
29 Nov RW, 66
30 Nov NJN, 268

Acknowledgments

BRINGING 365 MEDITATIONS into print has been a blessing and, at times, a challenge, as those of us at Blue Sapphire Books attempted to choose from four decades of my writings. Nelson Kane and Vania Kent were the chief architects of the selected passages, a task they approached with tender care and spiritual depth, spending months arranging and collating entries, corroborating and triple-checking references, with special citation assistance from Gina Lanzetta. A final edit of the entire manuscript was gently applied by Laurie Gibson.

The welcoming feeling of *Sacred Seasons* is the result not only of the ordering of entries, but also because of the beautiful design elements that Nelson wrapped into the text. From the four distinct images for each season, to the particular font chosen, and the colors of the cover, Nelson has imbued the pages with a sense of the holy.

My deep gratitude extends to each of them for this collaborative effort and work of love.

Beverly Lanzetta, PhD is a theologian, spiritual teacher, and the author of many groundbreaking books on emerging global spirituality and new monasticism, including *A Feast of Prayers: Liturgy to Holy Mystery*, *The Monk Within: Embracing a Sacred Way of Life*, *Radical Wisdom: A Feminist Mystical Theology*, *Emerging Heart: Global Spirituality and the Sacred*, and *Nine Jewels of Night: One Soul's Journey into God*. A monk of peace, she is dedicated to a vision of theological openness and spiritual nonviolence; her work has won praise for its wisdom, eloquence, and mystical insight and is considered to be a major contribution to what theologian Ursula King called "a feminine mystical way for the 21st century." Dr. Lanzetta has taught theology at Villanova University, Prescott College, and Grinnell College and has started a number of religious and monastic initiatives including the Desert Interfaith Church, Interfaith Theological Seminary, Hesychia School of Spiritual Direction, and the Community of a New Monastic Way. She is a much-sought-after mentor for the new generation, including the "spiritual but not religious" and new monastics alike, as she brings with her forty years of experience as a guide to answering the universal call to contemplation.

Made in the USA
Monee, IL
18 December 2021

86344736R00216